"*SOME MEN ARE MORE PERFECT THAN OTHERS* [is] soaring on the same ... updrafts as *Jonathan Livingston Seagull* ... A sort of Little Red Book of the bedroom ... It has already taken off!"

—*Time*

"A delightfully written book of warmth, grace and insight."

—George and Nena O'Neill,
authors of *Open Marriage*

"Wise, gentle, honest."

—Erich Segal,
author of *Love Story*

"The poet in Merle Shain wants to touch people. The liberated woman wants to help men to realize there are women out there who care for their vulnerability as much as their strength ... A modern, liberated woman writer has proved that she can also be soft and personal. And both men and women are benefiting from what she has to say."

—*Playgirl*

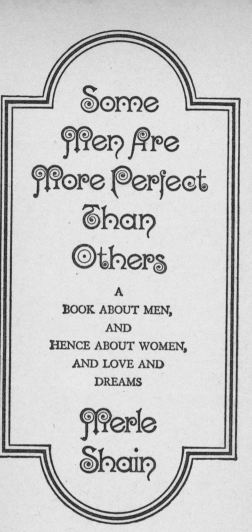

Some Men Are More Perfect Than Others

A
BOOK ABOUT MEN,
AND
HENCE ABOUT WOMEN,
AND LOVE AND
DREAMS

Merle Shain

BANTAM BOOKS
Toronto / New York / London

SOME MEN ARE MORE PERFECT THAN OTHERS
*A Bantam Book / published by arrangement with
Charterhouse Books, Inc.*

PRINTING HISTORY
Charterhouse edition published June 1973
2nd printing........July 1973
3rd printing.......August 1973
4th printing....September 1973
*A Selection of Insights Book Club, January 1974
Condensations appeared in* MCCALLS, READER'S DIGEST,
NEW WOMAN, BEAUTY, TEEN, CHATELAINE *(Canada) and*
SUCCESS *(Canada).*
A serialization appeared in the NEW YORK POST, *August 1973.*
Bantam edition published July 1974

Published simultaneously in the United States and Canada

*Bantam Books are published by Bantam Books, Inc. Its trade-
mark, consisting of the words "Bantam Books" and the
portrayal of a bantam, is registered in the United States
Patent Office and in other countries. Marca Registrada. Bantam
Books, Inc., 666 Fifth Avenue, New York, New York 10019.*

PRINTED IN THE UNITED STATES OF AMERICA

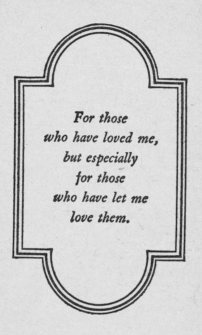

*For those
who have loved me,
but especially
for those
who have let me
love them.*

Contents

OLD MAN: *Love, now, love's another thing. Normally speaking, there's your four kinds. First off there's your light/fast: the sort as happens on a train or in swimming or a movie. Takes a lot of cheerfulness, does your light/fast. Then there's your heavy/fast. That's the sort as happens in a war. Happened to a nurse and me just beside the field-kitchen till the cook leaned out to cast slops. Or was that your light/fast? No, no. To her, maybe, as she soon afterwards proved out by going over the hill with the cook. To her it was just your old light/fast, but not to me and that's where you have your trouble. Then there's your light/slow. That's the best of the lot. Like floating, is your old light/slow. Like two swallows of wine on top of a pain pill. I only had your old light/slow once and she left, but that didn't stop it. Still get a touch of it now and then, especially when you can smell last year's leaf mold. Then there's your heavy/slow. Watch out for your heavy/slow! That's the sort as spoils bad habits. I know a man got so improved by your old heavy/slow that he married her. Haven't seen him since, of course, but as I've heard he's not dead.*

PART ONE

Love

CHAPTER ONE

Loving

There was an ordinary man once who worked for N.B.C. and fell in love with a French girl whom he met on a trip to Europe. The girl was very beautiful and it seemed unlikely that she would notice him, but he convinced her to come to America to live with him. Before she arrived, he moved to a coach house at a considerably larger rent than the bachelor apartment he'd lived in before, and he got a decorator to help

him make it look more impressive. For a while
things seemed to go well, and as he was connected with a show that went out of town regu-
larly, he took her with him across the country.
That was frowned upon by his superiors, but
still he traveled with her and then one day, for
that reason or another, he was fired, and shortly
after she left him, and he was all alone.

I remember this story and remember that it
was told to me by a much more attractive man,
and one who had a job and a wife, and I remember him saying, sitting cross-legged on a
velvet couch, "I went to see him at that coach
house, filled with all those paintings and an-
tiques, and he was lying there on the bed in the
dark, unshaven, cigarette butts everywhere, out
of work, in debt, alone, in total despair, and all
I could think of was how much I envied him,
really envied him."

IT IS HARD to write about men, because for a
woman to write about men is to write about
herself and the men who have been close to her,
and that is hard on everybody. There is a thin
line between being honest and being indiscreet,
and stripping by and large is considered better
form when it is done at the burlesque and not
between hard covers. But when I thought some
more about that ordinary man and his lost love
and the man who envied him, I knew that what

the first one had was emotional courage and the second was right to envy him.

Really splendid men have this courage and know that without it living is only housekeeping. You can tell them because they do as much feeling as they do thinking. It is not possible to think feeling any more than it is possible to hear blue, but many men clutch their hearts with their minds and stalemate their lives.

Feelings take you into uncharted territory from time to time it's true, but you almost always benefit from the journey one way or the other. We tend to think of the rational as a higher order, but it is the emotional that marks our lives. One often learns more from ten days of agony than from ten years of contentment, and while one might argue that the man who dared to love the girl who was beyond him was not courageous but simply ill-advised, it is just such sensible reasoning that keeps a lot of men safer but sorry. Proust said, "Happiness is beneficial for the body, but it is grief that ennobles the mind," and men who look at things his way likely figure they can't lose.

It's terrifying to care, of course, and the young man whom I once heard say to the girl whose hand he was holding, "Shit, I think I love you," in the ominous tones of someone declaring that he was coming down with the plague, probably put the fear that accompanies loving as graphically as it can be put. Men are supposed to fear loving because they fear depen-

dency and truly loving always involves surrender
of power, but there are men who are as much
afraid of being loved as they are of loving
others. "Some temptations are so great," Oscar
Wilde wrote, "it takes great courage to yield to
them," so most men opt for security in lieu of
feeling and call their decision maturity.

I KNEW A man once who loved a Chinese girl
way back when he was a college student, and
because he'd lacked the courage to marry her,
she'd married his best friend instead. The day
of her wedding she sent the man I knew a note
telling him that he was the only man she cared
for, claiming that she was marrying his friend
only because he wouldn't marry her himself.
Then she went to England on her honeymoon
where she threw herself under a subway car a
month after the wedding, and a day or two
later her new husband killed himself as well.

He'd lived with this for about twenty years
when I met him, but to the average onlooker
there were few signs of his tragedy, except perhaps that he had not married, preferring ap-
parently the company of a succession of big
blondes to any one girl. He'd prospered, though,
and led what most people would describe as an
interesting life, although it didn't seem to interest him very much. Some part of him always
remained uncommitted, until one day while

strolling to the drugstore from his penthouse apartment he happened to see a beautiful Chinese girl sitting by herself in a café, and though he kept on walking for a minute or two more he knew almost immediately that he would go back. "I ran back to her table," he said, when he told the story after, "not stopping for anything, not knowing what I was going to say when I got there, and I just started talking to her. I talked nonstop for close to two hours until finally she came with me to my apartment where she stayed for the next two months, leaving only to get her clothes."

When people heard the story, they loved it and everyone hoped they would make each other happy and that this Chinese girl would help him forget the one who went before. But loving someone because you failed to love someone else isn't the same as loving them for themselves, so after a while they parted. I'm afraid for him it was too late.

LOVING CAN COST a lot but not loving always costs more, and those who fear to love often find that want of love is an emptiness that robs the joy from life. Men and women who don't know love often feel they've missed the essential experience of life, so first-rate men find the courage to risk really getting involved with life, when the time is right, and while we all fear that we'll be hurt if we care, it's better to take a chance on love than to wish, when we've lost the chance, that we had.

AS ONE DOES with most things, one gets out of love what one puts into it, which is why women, who tend to give more time to love, get back a lot, and men, who leave their love to women to look after, get back less. In a love affair a very lucid lover might well say to himself, "More precious to me than your love for me is my love for you because that's mine." It is the lover, not the one who is loved, who gets the major share of the reward.

In Antoine de Saint Exupéry's children's story *The Little Prince*, the prince has one rose and two volcanoes on his planet and that is all. He loves his rose so much that he puts a fence around it to keep it from being destroyed by caterpillars, and he waters it every day. One day he is taken in a space ship to visit other planets, and when he gets to Earth he sees the many roses growing there. At first he is overcome by sadness because he thinks that he was foolish to have put a fence around his rose if there was nothing special about his rose after all. And then he realizes that he doesn't love the Earth roses but he does love his rose. And when he thinks about this for a while he realizes that he doesn't love his rose for its beauty, or for its uniqueness, but because he has watered it and cared for it and because it is his.

The value of a man is the sum of his commitments, or as Martin Buber put it, "I am what I do," and men who are loving make their women bloom. And because one of the best reasons for loving anyone is that they love you, men who understand that love is like the kind of flowers that grow more the more one gives away, are loved a lot, and men who do not water their gardens do not have roses to love.

IT IS HARD to resist a man who sings to you, or sends you violets, or braids your hair, and even an invitation to a pool game and a bowl of soup afterward can be magic when it comes from a man you can enchant. There once was a man who called a girl from the middle of a meeting and pretended he was checking with his answering service so the people with him wouldn't know he was thinking not of the task at hand but of something quite different, but she knew, and she had difficulty resisting him. It's marvelous to get telegrams inviting you to lunch or invitations to picnic on a bicycle built for two, and a lot of women spend a lot of time wishing they were Dante's messenger to heaven or at least the man next door's.

Beauty is as much in the ear of the listener as it is in the eye of the beholder, so there are

men women can be beautiful for and others for
whom it is simply not possible, as a tree falling
on a deserted island only makes a sound if
someone hears it fall. Women need men to love
them so they can love them back, and whatever
they seem to be saying about it at the moment,
women want very much to love.

CHAPTER TWO

Romantic Love

There is a love story I mean to write one day about a witty, charming man who was also very powerful, and his partner, who was not charming, but shy and repressed—although he was just as successful—and a young girl who worked for them. The charming man was wooing this girl at the moment and the love in the atmosphere turned the other man on, and so without really meaning to, he began to join in

the game, failing totally to understand that the
weapons he would be dueling with were those
his partner chose. The witty man began each
day by saying to his love such things as, "You
smell marvelous," and to make her giggle he
would invite his partner to smell her perfume
too. And then the shy man would leap up from
his desk, spilling his ink well and striking her
jaw with his head in his awkward efforts to
emulate the witty man's élan, and so it went
for several months, until one day she left the
first man for the second.

MEN ARE TAUGHT that women respect them for
their strength and that may well be true, but
they love them for their vulnerability and men
with tragic flaws are often loved the most of all.
Vulnerability is so seductive that some men
learn to feign it, but that is not the same.
Henry Miller wrote of a young man who came
to him for advice claiming he had persuaded
the woman he was trying to win to take off all
her clothes but then she would go no further.
And when he asked what he did wrong, Miller
turned to him and said, "You forgot to weep."

IT IS SAID that many men of our generation
were mutilated by the rationale that real men

don't show their feelings. Only a few men made it through the school yard and fewer still through the cocktail party circuit, and some of those who didn't are running off to Esalen to learn to touch and feel again, and perhaps this is heartening, if they don't learn to weep as they once learned to keep a stiff upper lip.

OUR TIMES ARE obsessed with finding fulfillment, so there are times when some people try too hard, and there are people who want to have the newest feelings just as there are those who want to have the latest model car. You can't play at love any more than you can be proud of your humility, or add water to your perfume and have it smell the same, but men and women both have been known to try.

Love is an infusion of intense feeling, a fine madness that makes you drunk, and when one is in love, life can be a succession of freefalls while working without a net. Love permits the lover to savor rare emotions and dangerous sensations, and because one is never so alive as when one is in love, and never so full of power, there are people hooked on love who wouldn't consider taking drugs.

AN ARTIST ONCE told me of a girl he'd loved a long time before. She was a Californian to whom he'd become engaged while working in her city, and when he returned home she stayed behind to finish her degree. They wrote to each other and made plans for their spring wedding and when he flew back to California she greeted him as before. Yet he sensed that something was different and closed his eyes so it wouldn't be true, until one night, two days before the wedding, she went out and didn't come back. When she returned in the morning, there was a man with her and she said she'd become involved with him in the artist's absence and found she couldn't give him up. The artist had no alternative then but to fly back home and try to lose himself in his work. Yet each day, as before, he wrote her a letter and promised her the moon and the stars, and although the letters came back unanswered, he wrote her one each and every day. Then, finally, when he had filled a large box with the letters he'd written to himself, he flew back to her city and, failing to reach her, went to speak to her parents instead. She was married, they told him, and happy, the mother of a small son, and they begged him to forget her and to look for someone else.

I asked him if he'd found someone else and he told me he was married, and happy enough, he thought. Then he said, looking across the room to nowhere, "I don't think I'd ever want to live like that again."

I've seen him five times in my lifetime and always we've talked of her, and once he made love to her sister and called her by the other's name. It's the thing that matters most to him and it's likely that it always will, and yet had he won her, it is possible that that would not have been the case.

One can get obsessions about people who give and then take away. Then what the lover doesn't have he seeks for obsessively until the seeking becomes a replacement for the loved object and is more satisfying still. And while it is never easy to stop loving once one has begun, there are men who want to love more than they want to have won. Unrequited lovers write poetry and build taj mahals, for which elusive lovers are the muses and kindle all the flames so there are poets who stoke their fires with love. Perhaps that's why there are an awful lot of songs that romanticize leave-taking, about people pulling out on a train, and perhaps that's why men who don't tiptoe out in the morning write a lot fewer songs.

THE ENERGY THAT runs from lover to lover is an electromagnetic ray that pierces through insensate anesthetized layers, expanding one's perimeters and making one young. Once wounded by love, we are open, so all our defenses escape, making it possible for us to see ourselves. And although that makes us terribly and gloriously vulnerable, it breaks our spirit's fast.

When you fall in love you feel wiser than others, and larger than life, and the things that happen when you are in love seem too important to be measured by ordinary standards, so lovers often risk everything on an emotional longshot that outsiders are sure can't pay off. The person you can't live without often is one you couldn't live with either, and because it is just as true that reality is what you believe it to be, sometimes a person who wants to believe his beloved beautiful and courageous causes them to be so by believing, making wishes fact.

Love often has more to do with the lover than it has to do with the beloved, and because it does there are people who prefer to fall in love with someone they hardly know. It can be more exciting to bounce love off an object than to deal with the reality of another whole human being. A fantasy love has a mystery that can be fleshed out with your own creativity, and you can make it do what you want it to, when you want it to, which isn't true of most real loves, at least not the ones I've known.

There is loving, of course, and being in love, and they are different again, which is why one will accept qualities in a lover one wouldn't accept in a spouse. Day to day contact has a way of causing the intensity of romantic love to dissipate and sometimes when you get the some-body you have yearned for, most of the magic vanishes with the pain. It's easy to want what you don't have, when you don't have it, and hard not to want something else when you do, so the big love in a lot of lives is the one that got away.

THEY DON'T HAVE romantic love with its em-phasis on nostalgia, tragedy and loss in cultures where children are raised by groups of adults instead of parents, so there are those who think romantic love is oedipal love, with the real love object being the image of the parent—ageless, perfect and unattainable—that the lover hungered for as a child. Falling in love at first sight is transference then, and well it might be, because romantic love—as in knights who served their ladies, as in people who are married but not to each other, as in star-crossed lovers of every kind—tends to be a love that is thwarted, if just slightly, keeping the lovers like those on Keats's Grecian urn, "for-ever panting, forever young."

There are men who are addicted to the magic of falling in love, and the ego-aggrandizing, intoxicating splendor of it all, and never learn that loving is better still. For them there is no help for a love that is losing its excitement but to fall in love again, with someone else—and when that too loses its intensity with someone else again. You can't maintain a constant state of falling in love, except through artificial means, but loving can go on forever and get better all the time.

LOVING ACKNOWLEDGES THE differences between people and helps each person to grow, and while it's unpredictable, and sporadic, because it's a process of exchange, generally lovers who are loving are more self-approving, yet less selfish, and happier in themselves. Romantic love seeks to possess the other person out of fear of loss, and romantic lovers want to give up everything for each other, merging themselves in the ones they love, until they have nothing left to give and their partners nothing left to love.

MEN WHO FEAR loving, fearing that love will require them to surrender power, often play at romantic love, demanding the surrender of their lover instead. But love when practiced that way, be it surrounded by however many hearts and flowers, is really just a mask for men's aggressions, a false peace at the best, and it has nothing to do with loving, nor will it ever do. Women are often trapped by their own romantic natures into believing that love means surrender, not recognizing that men who demand a woman's surrender are protecting themselves against her. And there are women who believe that a man is loving if he sends flowers, or holds hands, but that also is untrue.

Winning is conquering, any way you slice it, and for everyone who wins someone has to lose. When you surrender, you become someone's slave and since no one loves his slave or his master, that's the end of love. There's a bit of the poet in each of us and in some of us there is more than a bit, and most of us who have played the poet have also played the muse. But being the victim of your own fantasies or of someone else's is really still the same, and while a man with a variety of small moods and a capacity for ecstasy is easier to love than a dull one, it is not the same if he isn't on your side.

The best men have a touch of the poet, but probably just a touch, because there are some men who, even while they are writing poetry for you and beating their breast for you, are really saying more about themselves than they are about you or love, and while this is on the whole a lot nicer game to play than many, it is nevertheless a game. And if all that agony and all that ecstasy being swilled around with a ladle is really just a waltz around the room with his own ego, you could do just as well at the movies. Romantics tend to jump ship when the going gets rough, and women with men like that in their lives have to learn to manage alone.

CHAPTER THREE

Love
and
Making
Love

A young man in the Fifties learned that a successful pass in the backseat of his father's car was like making yards on the football field and that a sexual encounter was a game in which a male gained and a female gave away or lost. "It's a boy's job to ask and a girl's to refuse," a teacher told our class when I was fourteen, and mothers told daughters that they "trusted" them (a phrase daughters knew to mean that

their budding sexuality made their mothers
nervous and that mothers hoped their daughters realized that they'd be expected to bear the
burden of any transgressions by themselves).

Boys were "out for everything they could
get" and they didn't respect girls who were
"easy." And if your mother didn't tell you that,
the boys did themselves with phrases like "Did
you score?" and "Get much?" and "Does she
come across?" So girls quickly learned that
whatever boys said, they really wanted girls to
be virgins, and the only way to win the game
was not to play. Girls gave sex to get love and
boys gave love to get sex and conning girls was
the favorite indoor sport. The more attractive
a young girl was, the less she had to give away
and fellas were very clear about there being
nice girls and bad girls, nice girls being the
ones who blocked their tackles and held the line.

Boys played tennis and took cold showers and
joked that masturbation made you blind. It was
a bad time for the body and a good time for
guilt and fear, and anyone who put a hand on
anyone, including himself, was viewed as up to
no good.

The real game, of course, was not with girls
at all but with the guys, and many a young man
hardly got his sexual maneuver completed when
he hurried back to the soda fountain to tell his
buddies how big, how often and how long, and
sometimes he didn't bother with the girls but
went directly to tell the boys.

Size and staying power, the number of times one had "done it" or could "do it" were sources of great concern, because the game that wasn't with the other fellas was with oneself, and many a girl who saw a lot of action made the mistake of thinking that it was her body that the boys were after when, of course, it was their own.

And then one day the ballet of approach and retreat stopped and everyone grabbed a partner, and then a young man stopped talking, and after a bit he got engaged. The girl he chose, one of the "nice" ones, found it pretty hard sometimes to maintain their premarital "you can touch my left breast but not my right breast" morality and occasionally she slipped up. And then she worried about becoming pregnant and he worried about being caught and she got mad at being the custodian of their virtue—so they let up for a week or maybe two.

When they finally married, although a nice girl was now one who enjoyed sex, she'd spent so many years saying "no" it wasn't all that easy to say "yes," and there were nights when she had a headache, and nights when the children had the flu, and he was so busy getting ahead and thinking about the mortgage that he didn't always win her like in the movies. And when they went to bed she worried about letting herself go or he forgot to remember to think of something else, and afterward she said he was the best lover in the world and went to the bathroom and sometimes she cried a little when he turned over to sleep. Women trained by the Fifties knew very little about making love, only that you were supposed to convince the man he pleased, so they were often so busy performing they felt little pleasure themselves. And their husbands lying there in the darkness wondered why so often everything went wrong, and concluded that their wives must be frigid as they'd read so many women were.

BUT AFTER MASTERS AND JOHNSON, Women's Liberation, Dr. Reuben and the pill, nice girls who'd once said "no" and later "yes" to please their boyfriends started saying "yes" to please themselves, and men, who still considered a success something you stole off with in the night, felt like boxers whose opponents were bribed to throw the fight. And some of them repaired to fantasy, and elusive maidens one couldn't really have (because they were too married, too famous, or too distant, or because they were not asked), while others went to the office and never really came home again. Some men reverted to the old game of stalking women as they were trained. And some did it for ego more than for outlet or emotion, and some did it for the game. Some stalked women out of boredom, or curiosity, or rote. Some stalked them out of anger at somebody else or themselves. Some stalked them out of manners as they'd once pulled out a chair, and those who'd once done it for the soda fountain now simply played for higher stakes. The more prestigious the girl, the higher the man's score, which is why girls like Marilyn Monroe sometimes kill themselves when all the world seems to be at their feet.

I remember a very beautiful girl saying at a party to all who wanted to listen that she would be very upset if a man got into bed with her and then couldn't get himself together. And someone there asked why that would upset her and she said because it would prove that she wasn't attractive. And others tried to help her see that it might just as easily prove that the man was overworked, underslept, or overdrunk, but she would not be consoled. And then someone pointed out it was possible that he might not find her attractive, but that didn't mean she wasn't. And when they were finished, I asked her if she would be okay if he could laugh with her and maybe tell her a story and she brightened and said, "Yes" she thought she'd recover if it were a story about how beautiful she was, but she never thought of him.

AS WELL AS being pure and good, it was considered important in the Fifties to be pretty enough for love, so there were women who didn't think they were lovable and men who couldn't change their minds. Men found their bodies through women but women sometimes didn't find theirs at all, and women who didn't find their bodies often didn't find themselves, so they didn't love back much either, which was everybody's tragedy and still very often is.

There was a girl working near me several years ago who'd taken silicone injections hoping, presumably, to be more attractive to men. And all day long a parade of men cruised back and forth in front of her desk and all day long she scornfully turned them down. You catch a lot of flies with honey even though you may not want flies, and she of course was using the wrong bait. But she hated them for partially perceiving her and so spit in their collective face. Occasionally she went to bed with one, but on her terms and in her way, and as far as I know she hasn't loved anyone yet and it is possible that she never will.

THERE IS A fine line between seducer and stud, and men who require women to be instruments become instruments themselves. I can remember a Hungarian writer, whose novel concerning his own narrowly disguised sexploits made the best-seller list, once telling me of a girl who'd picked him up in the lobby of a hotel and suggested he come back to her room. And after everything was over she said she'd like to get some sleep and asked that he leave her and go back from whence he came. And I remember that as he told me he shook his head as he spoke, muttering over and over again, "She didn't even want to know my name."

It's been a hard time lately for some of these men and many are studying technique manuals with the urgency of students at Arthur Murray's. And although some of them are producing more female orgasms than they once did, many of them are doing it like little boys at the carnival—hitting the big thermometer to see how manly they are—and it's unlikely that anyone is much happier for their new learning.

ORGASMS REALLY HAVE very little to do with making love, and men who require their women to respond with a *petit mal* seizure that can be picked up on the Richter scale are not making love but asking for reassurance. It should be easier now not having to worry any longer about how often or how big, but men who are geared to competition are still concerned with making points. Orgasms are like calories or time or money, I suppose, of most interest to those whom life conspires to keep them from, but worrying about being multi-orgasmic is training for the Olympics and it's not likely people who are happy in bed spend a lot of time

counting. Passion can't be offered as an achieve-
ment, even though there are people who try,
and men who regard every act of making love
as a test have already failed. If a man can't put
his guard down in bed with the woman he
sleeps with, where can he put it down? Pleasure
is not the same as joy.

ONCE WE COULDN'T speak of sex and now we
can't speak of love, and strangers go to bed together instead of shaking hands. But many of
them don't like each other and still more don't
like themselves, and impotence has replaced
frigidity as the problem of the day. Women
used to trade sex to get love and communication, and sometimes they got it and sometimes
they did not, so more of them are trading sex
for sex itself these days, and because they are
trading for goods and services they are trading
sharper than before.

It's unbelievable, really, that a civilization of
docile women is just now getting around to telling men what pleases their bodies and I think
one must conclude from that that a woman who
is in bed with a man she cares about has more
than orgasms in mind. You can, after all, produce an orgasm yourself if that's what you
want, so we must go to bed for something more.

Love is lonely and poetic and mysterious and
whether we recognize it or not we climb into

bed wrapping our identities closely around us, not knowing what we want from each other, and fearing both that it might be too much and not enough. Each of us hopes to be acknowledged, succored and validated, and waits for the other to make the first move, and if we often accept an orgasm instead of what we hoped for, at some level we know the real gift is being known.

THE BEST KIND of men can laugh in bed and joke and play like children. They love the way their women smell and feel and taste, and if there are days when lovemaking works more for one than it does for the other they worry only if it lacks cheer. Women love men who stroke their hair, who lace fingers with them, and curl around them in the night, and men who cuddle as much after as before are thought to be the very best, and so are those who call the next day just to say hello. Most women would rather have someone whisper their name at the optimum moment than rocket with contractions to the moon, and ten minutes in bed with someone who appears to really know who you are, has been known to change a life.

PART TWO

Apart

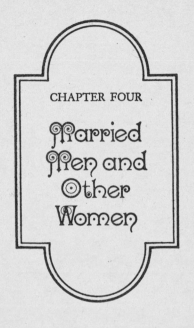

CHAPTER FOUR

Married Men and Other Women

I knew a man once who loved, and didn't want to love, and this duality made him behave very badly. Usually after he and the woman he loved, and feared to love, were very happy for a day or night, he'd do something horrible, hoping perhaps she'd take offense and with it take away his fears of surrender. Once he threw her out of a meeting over which he was presiding —simply stood up and hollered her name, or-

dering her to get out. And she, astounded, responded as if she'd been slapped, the tears
standing in her eyes, and looking stunned mur-
mured, "All right, I'll go then." But all the way
to the door she struggled to hold back the tears,
while trying desperately to think of something
funny to say, to protect him from the displea-
sure of those who'd heard him. She knew people
didn't like to witness another's humiliation, but
nothing funny came, and she was soon in the
hall, and then she was at home, face down on
her bed, where she remained for several days
before he called and said in a weary voice, "I
suppose you must hate me. I don't know what
made me do that. You'll never be able to face
those people again. What a terrible thing to do
to someone you love." And as one might imagine, she forgave him and went to the next meeting and everyone rushed to greet her, except
for him.

Sometimes he came to her house to end it all
and fell to weeping at the thought of all they
couldn't be to each other, and sometimes he
professed undying love and when she called him
"darling," he answered, "My name is Arthur."
Often she heard herself say to him, "Why won't
you let me love you?" although she knew he
didn't know the answer himself. And many people told her that it was perfectly clear to them
that he hated her. But she knew, having been
involved with married men before, that he

acted far too badly to hate her and that it must in fact be love.

IN MANY WAYS the love affair of a single girl with a married man (and this is much the same if it is instead an affair with a man who is a celebrity, or much younger than she, or perhaps might be homosexual, or is only passing through) is the contemporary equivalent of the kind medieval knights had with the ladies they served but could never possess, albeit in reverse. Because such an affair has an intensity fired by inaccessibility and suffering that marriage can rarely duplicate, and this is part of its appeal.

In the first stage, it is all ego-satisfaction, all warmth, heart-beating, phone-ringing, song-in-the-heart excitement, a dream world to enhance the real one, the moon to go around the sun. And then one day without warning the man finds he has a mistress not unlike his wife, two sets of commitments and expectations and a timetable with no nights for himself. What began as an oasis without responsibilities becomes a responsibility itself, and men who chose to diversify originally to have someplace where love was free usually disappear about this time.

But should he stay, then comes the time of boomeranging emotions and days when he would leave one and then the other, and days when he wishes they'd both leave him. And other days when both women feel lonely and seek his reassurance and he feels pulled in six directions and sick of the whole damn thing. And when he looks at the den he loves with all the books he asks himself, "What did she ever do to deserve my leaving her?" and when he goes to see his mistress to end it all, he falls in love again and, instead of leaving, begs for another week.

I once heard a man talking about his mistress, for whom he wanted to leave his wife, all the while beating his breast for fear of losing her, and weeping with the thought of hurting his spouse. And I can remember sympathizing with his dilemma, yet sensing that neither woman could win, because if he paid the price of his view of himself as a good husband and father for this new and special love, there would surely come a time when he would feel he had paid too much. And if his wife and children cost him that on which he'd set his heart, they too would pay, and pay in kind. And then I looked into his eyes and saw as clear as it could be that he already had what he wanted— the center of attention, and a new view of himself. And I realized even as I looked at him, and even as he wept, that somewhere deep inside of him he saw this as his finest hour.

ONCE I WOULD have said there is no way a wife can compete with a mistress who is always young and new and has time to brush her hair, but now I know a man rarely leaves one woman for another and even when he wants to, it's likely he'll mistrust his emotions and assess his opportunities' costs. A mistress has magic on her side, it's true, but no one really believes in magic, not even magicians themselves, and the wife has history on her side, and economics, and children and innocence, habit, inertia and self-respect. And many a man who wouldn't stay for her will stay for the image of himself as a good person, for his sailboat and his books, and because it is usually easier to stay where you are and do nothing, except when you must do something, anything at all. In that case, the mistress is simply a means of escape—like a parachute—essential to the skydiver's safety while airborne but extra baggage when on the ground. And many a woman who felt herself loved by a man when he had a wife finds she has less, not more, of him after he is free.

MISTRESSES ARE ADJUNCTS to marriages invented to fill its holes, so when the marriage goes, the mistress's job often goes too, because she really just existed to augment it. Sometimes a mistress keeps a bad marriage together by meeting its unmet needs, thus keeping the pressure off the wife, and there have been men who found

the way to tenderness through other women
and, having found it, took it to their wives.

When we love more than one person at the
same time, we are expressing various sides of
ourselves, so men with mistresses as well as
wives come to their mistresses to find themselves, not the women they seek. Married men
are like the balls on Bollo-bats soaring high off
the horizon secured by an invisible string,
which is why women often prefer them to
single ones, not recognizing that it is their tie
to the real world that fuels their flight. Married
men seem to give more of themselves sometimes, but usually they give what they themselves need, so if their marriage leaves room
for sex and excitement, or magic, or poetry, or
midnight dinners, that's what their other love
is likely to receive. And while that often pleases
her a great deal, especially in the beginning, it
isn't the same as getting what she would like.
Men don't come to see other women to help take
out the garbage and if they wanted to put up
the screens they would have stayed at home. So
mistresses tend to get a steady diet of whipped
cream, but no meat and potatoes, and wives
often get the reverse, when both would like a
bit of each.

MISTRESSES HAVE LOTS of excitement but very
little quiet joy and while they get to wear more

sheer nightgowns and make love more often by candlelight, usually they would trade their lot for a man who stays all night. Weekends are the worst time and holidays too and it is never easy to accept the fact that "her" expectations take precedence over yours.

Married men feel guilty about doing what they want, so the mistress is the one who pays when they decide to do the "right" thing. Many a candlelight dinner has been cancelled abruptly by a meeting of the PTA, and while the man who cancels dinner can feel morally upright and sacrificial too, the woman who is suddenly alone for the evening doesn't feel anything but blue. The wife's innocence usually protects her and keeps her calm but nothing protects the mistress, which is why she rarely lasts as long.

IT IS DIFFICULT to be involved with a man who reaches you when he needs you but whom you can't reach when you need him and the most difficult part can be hiding the fact that you don't think that's fair. It isn't easy to maintain a love, however special, when you don't share anything much besides a bed. And a man who has to lie to one woman to see another senses that his currency is somehow devalued with them both, while the woman who helps him lie soon starts fearing he also lies to her.

There are men who tell their wives they have

to stay late at the office and their mistresses that their wives won't let them out of the house so they can do what they wish. In any love relationship, the one who gives the least controls the show, so in a love affair between a married man and a single lady, his lack of time gives him the edge, and like the knights and their ladies but in reverse, the mistress ends up adoring him. The mistress feels she has the soul of the man and that's what really counts while the wife has the laundry—and who wants that? But the wife feels home is where the laundry is and takes heart from the fact that he's home at night.

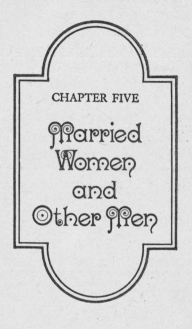

CHAPTER FIVE

Married
Women
and
Other Men

There was a girl once whose marriage was self-destructing and in her anguish she began to imagine another life, settling it upon the presence of a client of her husband, a bachelor architect who was nice-looking and talented but whom she hardly knew. At night when her husband was withdrawn and taciturn she wrote letters in her head to her imaginary lover, and sometimes she wrote them on paper and threw them in his car. The letters—more a soliloquy than a correspondence—were hand-lettered and decorated with pretty collages she'd cut from magazines and in them, as if embroidered, was her new set of dreams. The architect never responded and periodically, when she had a moment's lucidity, she'd write him an apology asking that he forgive her this flight from sanity and let her out the side door of his life. But he didn't answer her apologies either and after a couple of days or weeks she found herself writing him another love letter and dreaming her by now quite comforting dreams. When finally her marriage wheezed its last death gasp and she and her husband went their separate ways, she stopped writing the letters and she stopped dreaming the dreams, and when the architect finally came to see her she realized she'd left him the same day she'd left her husband, so there was nothing she could do but shake her head and offer him a cup of tea.

SOMETIMES WHEN NO gods exist to believe in we invent one so that we may have one in which to believe. Women need men to believe in because that's how they've been raised, and when they no longer believe in the one they've got they feel abandoned and terribly in need. In a society that says you are not important unless some man loves you it's crucial to know you are loved and many a man who wouldn't dream of leaving his wallet at the corner of Tenth and Main leaves his wife by herself much of the time. Marriage is considered to give women an identity but sometimes it costs them one instead, and many women who've been raised to believe they will find fulfillment through a man think the man has failed when he doesn't give them what they think he should.

Women whom the Fifties fashioned after Sleeping Beauty, expecting to be awakened with a kiss, often got kissed and then they married without fully waking up, so they think the prince who kissed them must be a frog disguised and question the man but not the myth.

The romantic myth is so strong that it survives the wear and tear of marriage by simply detaching from it and floating up on ahead, and women who are rather fond of the men they married, as well as ones who are not, go through life with a bag packed for the day when the shining knight on a white charger arrives, just in case he does.

IT'S NOT UNCOMMON for a married woman to say to herself or maybe to a friend, "I know what a good husband my husband is, and how good he is to the kids, and how successful he's been. We have everything we want. Then why do I feel there is something missing and why does that man across the room look awfully good to me?" But most of them, having said it, try to forget they thought it, and a few of them even remember it as something said by someone else.

Most of them throw themselves into housekeeping, cooking with every spice, and devote themselves to their children more than their children need, and they shop a lot because possessions make them feel loved, but they still dream of the perfect lover who is powerful, talented, passionate and true, and sometimes they think they've found him for a couple of weeks or a month.

Men who are married fall in love with their bodies but married women fall in love with their heads, so, rather like school girls, they tend to dream a lot. They dream about men they see when walking through Penn Station, and they dream about men closer at hand. And if they read something like George Bernard Shaw's love letter to Mrs. Patrick Campbell, they wish he wrote to them. There is an awful lot of repetition in housekeeping that can be done by rote which leaves the mind free and unoccupied for anyone to move in. Men have jobs and other challenges but women who are cloistered in their homes have fewer ways to test themselves, and that is why, I guess, some of them make a career of love.

In Mary McCarthy's short story "Cruel and Barbarous Treatment" a married woman is having an affair and she tries to keep it a secret for a while but she soon finds that she has to tell someone about it—if it is to be as satisfying as it should. She enlists a friend to listen to her and that works for a while, but soon she begins telling stories about her lover, dropping his name into the conversation, talking about him nonstop until she is flaunting him as one might flaunt an ermine coat, dragging it behind on the floor. And in time there wasn't anyone who didn't know about them, not anyone at all.

Women haven't been raised to love and be loved, they've been raised to adore and be adored. But proximity does terrible things to godlike qualities. Gods aren't supposed to get holes in their socks, or throw last night's underwear on the chair, and when they bathe they don't leave a ring. So sometimes a woman who picked a man because he was a good dancer or because she liked the way he ordered wine finds he doesn't seem as special once viewed at closer range.

AND WHETHER THEY'VE fallen out of love with their husbands for good reasons or for bad, or whether they still love them in their way, being seen as chief cook and bottle washer on the home front can cause a woman to seek an auxiliary relationship if just to have someplace where they can love as they choose. Women want to give love, not to have it expected, and sometimes husbands who need you very much don't need what you want to give. "Nobody loves anybody like anybody wants to be loved," Mignon McLaughlin wrote in *The Neurotic's Notebook*, and there is a lot of truth in that. But women often find their husbands don't love them for the things they value in themselves, and part of the charm of an affair is you can give what you want, and need only give if you choose. It's not easy to establish a relationship of parity in a marriage that wasn't begun on those terms, so women who want equality now, although they might not have realized that they did before, sometimes seek it in affairs. Men who don't totally possess you make fewer demands, and when you are not totally accessible, you have more control.

It's odd that women who find their husbands sexually demanding, as well as those who wish they did, both sometimes turn to other men, but sex that is sought after is different from that which is expected, so women whose husbands expect them to produce often lose out to men who do not.

THERE ARE WOMEN who are over-needed and so have affairs in order to have someone who thinks about their needs, and wives who aren't needed who have affairs in order to be useful once again. I knew a woman who used to leave her husband's home every morning a minute or two after he walked out the door and rush to her lover's where she busied herself making his bed. She brought a pot of soup for his lunch with her and she took his laundry home for her maid to wash every afternoon and she loved her lover very much because he let her use a part of herself her husband didn't need.

IT'S BEEN SAID that women earn love and men embezzle it, but it is probably more accurate to say that affairs are an assertion of self, whatever the self-asserting itself needs to say, and since affairs are no more perfect than marriages, women who turn to them to find perfection, often turn more than once.

Sleeping Beauty can't wake up herself, the princess in the tower can't unlock the door, so women who believe a man must save you, rarely think of saving themselves, although if they did they might also save the prince, which is why women tend to fall in love with the ski pro when they are in St. Moritz and a beachcomber when at the beach. The man who is in charge of the environment is the prince of that domain, and women who always need a man to make them feel worthwhile, choose the man who has worth in the neighborhood, but often he is somebody she wouldn't want back home.

A psychiatrist makes a good prince if you don't feel too sure, and so does an obstetrician, or a teacher, or a boss.

Men understand that women are drawn to power as surely as they understand that fireflies are drawn to light, but they don't understand that however powerful they may be they are never powerful enough. A politician once told me that whenever he gave his "Let's storm the bastions" speech women came out of the woodwork and threw themselves at his feet. Then he began another story about his secretary whom he was trying to convince to leave her husband and marry him. He'd taken her to Paris and brought her expensive gifts, hoping that would convince her that the better future was with him. When I suggested he trade even with her husband giving her a better chance to judge both men on their merits, and him the certainty that it was really him she chose, if she did, he said very simply, "I am afraid to do that, afraid that if I do, I'll lose."

IT'S TOO BAD that men think women want bangles and plaid mink coats because while they are giving women those things they are too busy to give them what they need. I once heard a jeweller say that the best towns for jewellers are those in which there is a lot of illicit love because men who feel guilty give their wives a lot of gifts. Men who've diverted their emotional energies elsewhere traditionally offer their wives placeboes of the monetary kind to keep them from noticing they aren't getting what they want, but women who are bought off know they've been sold out.

Gifts and money, insurance policies, and the house in your name tell some women they are loved I suppose, but it isn't what most women really want, even those who take all that they can get. Women get involved with men after marriage for the same reason they get involved with them before, because they want to love. When married men fall in love with other women they always hope they won't care too much but married women in the same position almost always hope they will.

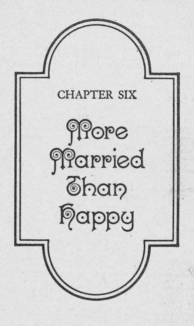

CHAPTER SIX

More Married Than Happy

Marriage is supposed to do everything, like Duz, which is more than half its problem. It is said to save us, define us, give us purpose, keep us from loneliness, and incidentally balance our diet and wash our socks, and when it doesn't, we get divorced.

Programmed by Hollywood and our parents' dreams of immortality, our visions of marriage are ephemeral whimsies that take us no farther

than the altar. And failing to note that the difference between movies and real life is that
movies end as the couple walks off into the sunset, while marriages just begin there, most of
us jump in blinded by romance and good intentions, hoping for the best.

We want to be together all the time, so we
lock ourselves away in the love nest and begin
to sacrifice individuality for "the relationship,"
personal friends for mutual friends, and evenings with the boys for nights in which both give
up what they would like to do for activities
neither really wants. We want to be each other's
best friend and constant companion, confidante
and confessor, bed partner and golf partner,
and forsake all others to that end. Until after a
short while we start to feel constricted and less
sure of who we are. Soon exclusivity leads to
dependency, jealousy and insane fears of aban-
donment, and sensing each other's vulnerabil-
ities, we tell each other the lies we think the
other wants to hear instead of what we really
feel.

IN MOST MARRIAGES, there is the neat one and
the messy one, the punctual one and the late
one, the dependable one and the unreliable one,
the exploited and the exploiter. One partner
dances and the other holds the string—one is
the puppeteer, the other the puppet, and some-

times they switch about. In time, they carve each other out, and it's no longer possible to tell where one ends and the other begins. They even speak in the same voice.

And sometimes, when the polarizing process has gone to the furthest extreme, partners transpose personalities, the strong one encouraging the weak, until the weak one grown strong threatens to leave, and the strong one capitulates, starting another round. Saints need sinners, winners need losers, sages need fools, and marriage practiced as we know it has a way of making each for each.

I ONCE KNEW a man who arrived at his office every morning cursing his wife and muttering to himself about what terrible things he had to live with and what he suffered at her hands. One morning he arrived yelling, as he came up the stairs, "You know what she did this morning? Threw her egg at me, and it hit the wall. A fried egg is on my kitchen wall. It was still there when I left. I'm not going to clean it up. It can stay there forever for all I care." On another morning he entertained the coffee break complaining that his wife wasn't speaking to him, because the night before, when he was reading in bed, she'd nudged him a bit with her hip as she got into bed, and he, not wanting to be disturbed, had body-checked her "just a bit."

So she fell out of the bed and hurt her back, and he was aggrieved by her bad mood in the morning.

The whole office listened to his stories, and if they didn't always side with him they shared his view that his marriage didn't work and that he suffered considerable pain because of that. Then one day he announced that his wife was going to England to visit her parents for two months and he hoped she would never come back. When she left he was positively euphoric for a couple of days and then grew subdued. Occasionally he invited one of the girls in the office to join him for dinner but one wouldn't say he was making hay while his wife was away. He seemed hardly to care if he had company or not, although there was one girl whom he invited more than once. She was a young girl who smiled a lot, and once before she'd taken his wife's side on the morning when he'd told everyone how he'd knocked her from the bed. The young girl was a delicate person and seemed almost to cringe when he bellowed, but she went along to dinner with him several evenings. And then one morning he arrived, bristling as he used to in the days when his wife was at home and marching up to the girl's office, he slammed her door until her pictures rattled, and yelling so loud his voice carried over the partitions, shouted, "I could never live with you, you've got no malice."

"In every marriage there is the one who loves

and the one who lets himself be loved," Somerset Maugham wrote, and there are people who prefer to have someone to hurl themselves against than to have someone who is on their side.

WE MARRY FOR all the wrong reasons, and often we marry the wrong person as well, and even when we chance to marry someone we continue to like, having the notion that our mate should be our everything can make the marriage go awry. Some part of each of us is a dark forest and no one can follow us there, so every marriage has a little pocket of unmet needs. Often those who know us best also know us least of all, so one can be imprisoned by another's needs and expectations almost as easily as by one's own.

I knew a girl once with blond hair and opalescent skin who was from an upper-class family and who was married to a man who thought those things more important than they were ever meant to be. His own background was very different and he was not as proud of it, so having her beside him made him feel better than he really was. She admired his intelligence and his ambition, two things she felt she lacked, and hoped by having him to talk for her she wouldn't have to speak as often for herself. He loved her for being what he hated himself for

not being, so he spent a lot of time putting her
down to show himself he was better still, and
she found that having him protect her didn't
make her feel much safer because she still
needed protecting—but from him.

WE MARRY TO grow up, to escape our parents
and to inherit our share of the world, not knowing who we are and who we will become, so it
is left to marriage to make it clear which ones
of us are growing in the same directions and
which are ships meant to have passed in the
night.

Women who look to men to define them are
defined by their man's limitations as much as
by his strengths. If you let a man tell you what
you believe, you never really know it for yourself, and if what he believes isn't right, what
you believe is wrong as well. And when he fails
to perceive the things you love best about yourself, you have less in yourself to love. Nobody
should let one person define him—man, woman,
or dog. Marriage doesn't work when it cuts us
off from finding who we are and defining ourselves for ourselves.

The word "marriage" connotates for many
the kind of life mother had, so lots of couples
end up with an arrangement neither really
wants. He makes her his mother and she makes

him her father and while that rarely works, it is all they know, so it's what they get.

Should I tell you, perhaps, of a girl I knew once long ago, long ago when she was me, who put a husband through law school and kept house in between, and when there was time left over, which there wasn't most of the time, she went to the university also, and got a degree or two herself. And though she had to run full speed some days just to stay in the same place, she did what her husband expected of her—or what she thought he expected of her—before she did what she wanted to do. So on most days she cooked one of her mother's recipes when she came home from her job, and scoured all the bottoms of the copper bottom pots, and sometimes she didn't get to her assignments until eleven or twelve at night but she never asked him to help her with a dish, feeling that her right to go to school herself was a dispensation from the gods that could be withdrawn if ever she complained. And when the next stage of life came and she was now to stay at home and polish little boots, she found there weren't as many hours in the day as there had been before, so those hours she'd once scraped and saved for herself were the first to go. It was hard for her to stay at home, and not go out each day into the world. She missed the fight, she missed the raspberry season, she missed the changes in the weather. Sometimes she

called her husband six or seven times to ask
when he'd be home, and woke the baby up just
to talk to him, although he didn't have a lot to
say. Fortunately (or unfortunately, depending
on your point of view) she wasn't as adaptable
as love decreed a good wife to be, so she never
made the transition from person to housewife
and mother, giving up herself, although God
knows she tried. And her husband, who'd been
trained to think there was nothing as loving as
something from the oven, thought he'd got a
dud, and wasn't any help. Then one day, the
census taker came and asked her if she worked,
and she sat down on the floor and cried after
answering, "Like I never worked before," and
later on, if not the same day, they decided on
divorce.

MARRIAGES IN WHICH there is an inequity of
needs can't work, so those based on the premise
that a wife's needs are met by meeting her husband's are doomed before they start. And
whether the worst offender is the woman who
rushes to give up her needs hoping to please the
man, or the man who accepts her sacrificial
gifts, they both pay for it a thousand times. We
expect women to do what their mothers did and
to do what they were trained to do too, so
women expect too much of themselves, and

often lead their husbands to expect too much as well.

It is not possible to be the kind of wives our mothers were because the world is different and so, therefore, are our needs. Most of us are better educated than our mothers were and abilities that are not used clamor to be used, festering when they are not. High-rise buildings and matriarchal suburbs leave us isolated as well as trapped, and labor-saving devices such as frozen foods rob us of our creativity as well as our family's respect while returning to us time we have to look around to fill. Child-raising is more difficult when fathers are rarely around, and that all adds an extra strain. Men often want to have children, like writers who want to have written more than they want to write, so after they father children, they leave them at home while they go elsewhere for their lives. It's a lot harder to be married today, for women especially, and if we add the burden of what was expected of them once to the burden of what is expected of us now, the burden is too great.

Since the problem is with our expectations rather than with marriage itself, a lot of people are living together today hoping that way they can start fresh. If no one says the word "marriage," it's easier to evolve a plan of your own. There isn't any single formula for marriage which all couples should find right, and at-

tempting to run your life by your parents'
standards or your neighbors' is bound to run
aground. Marriages should be as diverse as the
people in them are, which means some will be
of one kind, and some totally different still. And
those who don't want to love, honor and obey,
should be able to promise each other anything
they choose, without having to ask anyone what
they think of that, particularly themselves.

THERE IS A difference between needing and
wanting and a difference between wanting and
needing and loving, and both partners have a
right to what they need, although not always to
what they want. Each partner has a right to
one life and to that life he has the sole right. He
hasn't a right to his spouse's life, and he hasn't
a right to his child's, but he has a right to his
life, and no one should interfere with that.

It is not possible for one person to meet all of
another's needs and marriage partners who expect this soon find each other wanting. When
people don't meet all of our needs, they are not
always rejecting us—more often, they are saving themselves—and in a good marriage this is
perfectly all right. People who are loving toward each other set up their marriages so that
it is possible for both partners to get what they
need from life and so that no one is expected

to give up his needs to meet those of his spouse. And when their partner meets one of their needs they accept it as a gift, instead of viewing each unmet one as if it were a betrayal.

OUR TIMES ARE obsessed with finding fulfillment, so they are times of more than the usual strain between men and women and a good deal of that strain is blamed on marriage, although it should not be. There was a movie a season or two back called *Lovers and Other Strangers* which had a scene in which a son tries to tell his Italian father that he and his wife of only a few years have decided to get a divorce because, as he puts it, "We feel there must be something more." The father, not understanding what that has to do with anything, answers, his eyebrows raised for an explanation, "We all feel there must be something more," to which his son replies, "Then why don't you leave Mom and get out and get it, Dad?" And the old man shoots back, "Because there isn't something more!"

Perhaps it was easier for our parents to live with the needs their marriages didn't answer when they believed they would get their reward in heaven. And some of them believed that there was somebody with a big book sitting up there somewhere recording every sacrifice they

made. But it's the fly now, pay later world we
live in today, so most of us want our rewards
right now.

Our parents dreamed of better jobs and
larger houses, more money and more status, but
we dream of less tangible things—even if we
don't know what they are ourselves.

The Arabs had a saying in the eighth century
that translates roughly, "A hungry man is
happy because he believes in food, and therefore his desires are simple enough that he can
believe they might be satisfied." George Jonas,
the Canadian poet, wrote a poem from that
saying that goes, "The happy hungry man believes in food. The happy homeless man believes
in home. The happy unloved man believes in
love. I wouldn't mind believing in something
myself."

It's in the fight, in the striving, in the moun-
tains unclimbed that fulfillment lies, so if you
have nothing to strive for, you have nothing to
make you happy. When it comes to "for better"
or "for worse," "for better" is often harder on
a marriage.

PART THREE

Together

CHAPTER SEVEN

Getting It Together

Whether you marry for practical reasons or marry the person you fall in love with, you still have to make it from there to loving if marriage is to work. Loving isn't easy and many never get the hang of it, so they feel that love has failed. But those who do learn have better lives, and if you know them you can see that, although they aren't that easy to spot. And who's to say what form love should take.

Once a man I knew was in an accident and got burned from head to foot, and I remember going to the hospital, steeling myself for an unpleasant sight—bringing flowers with me and sympathy, if very little else. And when I was there, another girl came to see him—one who knew him longer than I—and she asked how long he intended to lie around feeling sorry for himself and why he wasn't working and if he didn't have anything useful that he could do. I remember thinking her incredibly cruel until I noticed that he was sitting up when she left though he had been lying down for me, and shortly after, he was actually working, muttering to himself, "I'll show her. She'll see. Wait till she sees this." So I concluded that she loved him better than I did, because by making it necessary for him to show her she made it possible for him to show himself.

LOVING SOMEONE MEANS helping them to be more themselves, which can be different from being what you'd like them to be, although often they turn out the same. When you ask someone to live through you and for you, they warp like a Japanese tree to suit the relationship which you are, and cease to be what you chose them for, that is, cease to be themselves. So men who are loving like as much as they love, and somehow they find the courage to let their partners grow in the direction they need to grow, even if that contains the risk that they might grow away.

Good people can't be possessed and those who can one never wants for long. No one gives you security—you have to do that for yourself. Love can't buy happiness, marriage can't buy happiness, only happiness can buy happiness, so it is also unwise to think of finding happiness in terms of roles.

Being someone's wife or being someone's mother or even being the best plumber or the best brain surgeon may give you some security for a while, even for a long while, but you always have to be ready to find it somewhere else when the time comes, and it tends to come oftener than one would have thought.

Santayana wrote in an essay entitled "Cloud Castles" about the virtue of impermanence, pointing out that clouds are all different and that, as well as there not being two clouds the same, the clouds themselves keep changing and hence are never the same for very long. Marriages work best when both the people in them allow each other to be like those clouds, delighting in each other's changes. And those who attempt to find security by eliminating inconsistencies eliminate the miraculous with the same deft hand.

There is no security in a relationship that tries to hold on to what was, nor is there security in the one that dreads what might be.

There is only security when we accept what is here now, with its limits and its surprises, and when it goes, in accepting what comes, as we would turn over the pages of a book.

ONE'S TWENTIES SPENT learning something about oneself as well as something of those around one gives one a better idea of what one will become. And couples who marry after most of their growing is done aren't as likely to grow in opposite directions as soon as the knot is tied.

Women who come to know something of their own sexual natures before they marry make more responsive wives, and what a man loses in his mate's innocence he ought to pick up in her ability to forget about herself and think of him. The end of virginity as a value is part of the demise of the view of women as possessions instead of people—like pots fresh from the factory in which no one's yet baked. I've never been sure what men thought they were getting when gifted with someone's virginity, but I doubt that many of them will miss the awkwardness, self-righteousness and self-obsession that comes with it as well.

Men as well as women who've had some time to try out different styles of life after they leave home should do less fantasizing once married, having a better idea what they seek. And being clearer who they are themselves, there'll be less searching for someone to fulfill and define them and less finding them wanting when they don't.

Good marriages seem to function something like a buddy system—the people in them swim in their own waters but keep a protective eye on each other, and should the whistle blow, turn up quickly to hold each other's hand. It's more important today than ever before to know what your priorities are because life links us with more people than our hearts can hold, so men who know what they will go to the wall for, as well as for whom, are the ones whom it is nicest to be married to, presuming you're the one they have at the top of their list.

THOUGHTLESSNESS IS THE weapon men most often use against women, such as promising and defaulting, and chronically being late, and withdrawal—a form of passive warfare as lethal as letting go in a tug-of-war. Women prefer men who get angry to ones who go quietly out the door. And as for those who say, "Yes, dear, whatever you say, dear," while doing exactly as they please—they are the worst there is. It's impossible for men and women who love each other not to hurt each other now and then, but most women would settle happily for a man who tried not to cause the same hurt twice.

Two people's needs don't dovetail all of the time and very soon in any relationship partners are asked to meet needs the satisfaction of which does not particularly please them. Men seem to find this harder to do than women, perhaps because they've been raised so often by sacrificing mothers who gave them the idea that pleasing themselves is what pleases women most. And so they tend to consider women to be nagging when women raise concerns that they don't share. Some men meet their partner's needs because they feel they should, and some do it as a form of insurance so theirs will be met on other days, but neither of these reasons is as good as doing it because you want to see the woman in your life happy, and women know which is which.

PERHAPS THE MOST important thing in any relationship is keeping the lines of communication open. Though this sounds simple, it can be difficult at the pace of life most of us keep, and lots of people who have lived together for years have to make an appointment with each other if they want to talk. There are lots of ways of communicating, of course, and you can sometimes say as much with the laying on of hands as with a three-page letter sent in triplicate and double spaced. But letters are nice too, and so are fireside chats, and a half hour in bed when the lights are out can make everything right with the world.

Some of us have trouble finding words for what we mean, or we speak in cryptic messages hoping the other person will figure out what we mean and rush in to save us from ourselves, and when they miss the message we feel isolated and alone. It's very important to decode your own messages, like saying "I feel angry" instead of kicking the cat, and people who learn to do this find they are misunderstood less often and, as a fringe benefit, are clawed by fewer cats.

The best men are those who put their cards on the table when something is bothering them, and if possible do it quietly, not blaming anyone, and if they're faced with a hysterical partner, who is not herself, identify with what she feels even when they can't make head or tail out of what she says.

Women find it very hard to express anger, feeling perhaps that men will lose their love for them the moment they are anything but sweet. But men can usually deal with anger more easily than they can deal with guilt, and women who shout a lot can be shouted back at, which is hard to do with one who weeps.

A man once did something horrible to a girl I know that made her feel awful for a while, but when she pulled herself together she wrote him a long, very definitely worded letter telling him just what she thought. It was a letter in which she tried to make things clear but at the same time not to whine, and it likely did the trick because he sent her back a note that read, "I thought I'd lost you for all time. Was awfully glad to find you were just pissed off."

If you never get angry you never know where you stand, and it is also possible that you provoke people into worse and worse behavior just to get your attention or to make sure that you care. People who are loving tell each other what they feel, even when they don't expect the other to share their point of view, and if they don't always get what they want, at least they know what they can expect, and that, while it isn't everything, is at least a start.

GOOD MARRIAGES SEEM effortless to those on the outside but a lot of care goes into them, like cultivated flowers that look like they grow wild. Sweet peas have to be weeded and mulched and given exactly the right amount of water and sun, but when they get all that, they turn into a froth—and marriages given what they need do so as well.

The love you didn't make yesterday you can't make today and couples who make the mistake of living for the future often let the present slip by them on the way. The day you spend hoping, the day you spend waiting, the day you spend in despair, is a day in your life as much as the tomorrow you hope for, but which may never come, so betting today on tomorrow is always a bad bet. If you spend your life saying "if only I" every time you let one "if only I" slip by you, another three take its place, until your whole life is nothing but a collection of regrets.

Marriages should be for the people involved and not for the material goals one might store up, the things one might do if one gets the promotion, the people one hopes will be impressed. And if it isn't for the people involved in it—who needs it?—whatever else it is.

The forms of marriage are in transition, and it is possible that marriage will not last, but great marriages can have large and generous forms of being and here's hoping that we'll get some of those because those are the kind we need.

CHAPTER EIGHT

Today and Tomorrow

There are men who value women because they are handy things to have around. And there are men for whom women are ammunition for the cockfight. The current female archetype held in high esteem by men is the woman who can do everything—and does. If she plays the violin in a philharmonic somewhere, has three marvelous kids all born by natural childbirth, and keeps her house in the manner of *House and Garden* magazine, she isn't in an appreciably better position than the woman who is seen as a Hefneresque sex object, if it's for that that she is valued. And inside most such ladies is a small thin person signaling wildly to get out of her with-it outfit into a terrycloth robe to see if she is still valued when she underachieves.

WE SAY WE marry for love in North America, but many a man thinks yelling, "Is dinner ready?" is the same as saying "I love you." And lots of women who really want love and communication ask for a mink coat instead. There are libraries full of books about women who sold their souls for romance and got instead dishpan hands, and bars filled with men wondering why the more successful they become, the worse their marriages become as well. Underneath many marriages are business deals in which the partners, although they pay lip service to love, have really contracted to secure certain goods and services, and love is little more than never having to say you're horny or hungry.

Our society smiles on a man who marries for sex but disrespects him if he marries for money, yet encourages a woman to marry for money but considers it absurd if she marries for sex, not recognizing that all marriages based on the exchange of services are in trouble when the service is no longer required.

A man who is considered a good catch if he comes with a big ring, and a good husband if he is a good provider, isn't missed much if he leaves a big will or big alimony payments. And a man who buys a bed-mate often buys two or three. Sometimes it is out of our needs that we create each other, which is why a man crawling on his belly in the desert always wants water, but it is also why after he has it, he wants theater tickets, or in any case something more. The kind of wife who is perfect when one is twenty may not be so perfect when one is forty and very often a man who chooses a functional wife when young, wishes he'd chosen a luxury model later on.

SOMETIMES THE SERVICES people hope marriage will secure for them are the obvious ones and sometimes they are more obscure. Women have been known to marry to have the role of wife and mother as often as to have a roof over their heads, hoping to hitch a free ride on the man's identity, thinking his success will make them a success as well. And men sometimes choose women whose beauty or prestige makes them feel important because they really doubt that they are, but this kind of man, once he's married, finds living with a successful wife makes him feel less important instead of more.

I once overheard a man at a party saying to those around, "See that girl over there, she's with me, she is in movies, isn't she grand?" But when those people whom he'd told went to talk to her themselves, he whispered to her when he thought no one was listening, "I don't want you to talk about your work. You're drawing too much attention to yourself"—by which he meant "away from me." When her status accrued to him, he thought it was a good thing, but when it accrued to her it was bad, because he didn't love her—only wore her, really, like a boutonniere, and because to him she was just a decoration, he probably didn't understand why what he said wasn't really fair.

A woman who marries a man to give herself an identity tends to choose the most powerful man she can find, so she often marries an over-achiever, thinking that his success will make her a success as well. One always thinks that very successful men will be more generous and kind, but over-achievers of either sex are driven people, hoping to win love from every source, and a woman who chooses that kind of man is usually neglected for his work, and ends up with less identity than she had to start.

WE HAVE A way of changing our view of the ideal woman every decade, so many women born in the mid-Thirties had their lives subdivided by the ambivalence of a society that educated girl children no differently from boy children, then admonished them against using their education except to further their husbands' careers. And when finally they accomplished this, paradoxically urged them out of the house, warning them of the dangers of stagnating and turning into little brown hens.

All of that, as everyone knows, has resulted in a lot of thirty-five-year-old women—who once married and raised a couple of kids and spent their extra time making long skirts for all the tables like the magazines told them to—who now aren't sure what to do with tomorrow, and it's too late for them to be doctors and not soon enough for them to die. And rather too many of them have husbands who seem to be saying, "Who asked you?" when told of all their sacrifices—like how they gave up the chance to be a singer, and while that shouldn't surprise anyone, it doesn't seem quite fair.

Perhaps the old view of "Me breadwinner, you hausfrau" worked for our grandparents, when people obligingly popped off before boring each other to death, but it won't work any longer because we are living too long and divorce is needed today to do what death accomplished more economically before. It costs a lot to have a woman pick up your socks every day, and on the whole, having a full-time housekeeper for a wife and a part-time mistress for diversion is more expensive than having a full-time mistress for a wife and a part-time charlady for the chores. Even when you have to be the charlady yourself on occasion it is cheaper, and a man who wants to be enchanted in his fifties by the same woman he married in his thirties will have to see that she gets the right nourishment along the way.

Women who are alive and ticking are more interesting to live with than ones who are trapped and resentful, and two people making dinner while telling each other about their day can be as happy as two people at the movies or sitting together by the fire. Masculine strength simply doesn't have anything to do with who cuts the cucumber for the salad, and men who know this and adapt will survive this and other storms.

There are women who want to stay home who are being urged to get out and get themselves jobs, and women who want to work who are being kept at home, and they are all in the same boat although they mistakenly think they're not. The woman in the terrycloth robe who wonders if she'd still be loved if she didn't do everything just so, and the woman who can't do anything anymore because it's been such a long time since she had a chance, are both victims of the needs of men.

Loving hasn't anything to do with who does what for whom, and when it has, it isn't love. Women want to be valued for what they are instead of what they do. The best men want women to do what they need to, and need them to do what they want to do, which is to say women love to do things for men, the things they love to do.

IT'S A DIFFICULT time to be a man vis-à-vis women, so it is not surprising that many men have opted out. Like knights gone off to the crusades. And some of these are at the office and some are in the locker room and some are on safaris stalking women and other prey, but men who really like women are still hanging in there. And while they may be confused by the emerging twentieth-century female's demands, and wonder if wisdom lies in trying to understand her or in beating her about the head and shoulders, they are enjoying the experience and even their confusion, and they will be okay.

The best kind of men have a certainty in themselves that isn't done in when countered by a certainty in their women, and they are much adored. This kind of man isn't diminished by a woman who wants to work or flirt or think, nor

will he let a woman trade a piece of her freedom for a piece of his. Men who lack this belief
in themselves often fear and dislike women, so
they worry a lot about keeping the upper hand,
not recognizing that masculine strength has
nothing to do with ruling. If women have to be
small so men can be big in their own eyes, nobody much is fooled, and men who require this
lose out in other ways.

THERE IS NOT much to be said for the business
of the male having to be superior except that
it's a terrible strain. For men to be superior,
women have to be inferior, which requires a
lot of play-acting for both parties and never
seems to work. And an awful lot of men would
likely trade their male supremacy for a chance
to be accepted as they actually are.

Much of women's resentment toward men at
the moment is related to their notion that men,
since they are supposed to be superior, should
meet all their needs, and that is a pretty heavy
trip to lay on anyone and generally leaves men
feeling they've been charged with the national
debt.

Many a superior woman spends her lifetime
looking for a man who is more superior instead
of for one she likes, not realizing that demanding that a man be superior isn't much different

from demanding that he be rich. Men who are required to be superior will always be insecure, and a man who feels his wife should get her identity from his success rather than from her own finds himself having to run all day just to keep up with her demands. Impotence for one is always impotence for both, and men and women who don't recognize this inadvertently become the killers of their own best dreams.

A man who insists that his woman lay her head on his shoulder and lean on him, doesn't realize that if she takes her feet off the ground in this position and hangs on she will be a drag. Psychiatrists are plagued by men who want to know what to do with dependent wives who can't make a move without them, and rising young copy writers are plagued by men who call them after dinner parties to confess that they wish their wives were as interesting and ask if they might have time to meet for a drink. Many marriages between two people become marriages between one and a half very quickly, and people who fear invented the "his and hers" towel culture and are now thrashing around inside.

Women who suffer loud and lengthily and weep copious tears make men feel guilty, beleaguered and anxious to get to the door, and little-girl acts of coyness get them somewhere in the short run but cost them dear in the long. Not only do women despise the men they catch with them and turn them into Jiggs, but men who are manipulated and patronized long enough declare emotional bankruptcy and give up the store.

One of the reasons men fear loving is that they don't want to take responsibility for another total human being. The kind of woman who loves out of need and desperation frightens even the best men off, and women who want someone around they can count on won't feel better until they can count on themselves. The whole superiority-inferiority, passive-submissive business is a bum steer. Women who don't expect the men in their life to give them fulfillment on a silver platter aren't as likely to hold them responsible when it isn't so easy to come by. And men who are not expected to be superior, only human, generally accomplish both more of the time.

REALLY SPLENDID MEN have an acceptance of themselves and a generosity of mind and spirit, and that makes them easier on themselves and easier on those around them, and sometimes they are strong and certain and sometimes they are not so sure, but they don't worry about their inconsistencies and allow women theirs as well.

The best men can play all the parts, child and

father, lover and loved, and play them all in every encounter. There are men who look after and men who need caring for, but one rarely finds them both in one. A man who is paternal but not patronizing, childlike but not childish, is extra special and usually ends up owning the world.

CHAPTER NINE

Being True

La Rochefoucauld said, "There are good marriages but no delicious ones," and perhaps he was right. It's not easy to stay excited about the only game in town. Winning someone is really more fun and ego satisfying than pleasing them —and who ever talks about that. Besides, an adolescence spent conning girls to rip off doesn't get you off to much of a start.

Our society is ambivalent about sexual fidelity, jointly teaching us that sex is good for you and that it is terribly wrong, so we hold up fidelity as a value while teaching the virtues of sexual expertise. Infidelity is seen as neurotic, normal, evidence that the marriage is in trouble, and/or that it really swings, and most of us understand that asking someone to be faithful to us for a lifetime is asking to be lied to, yet we do so anyway and close our eyes.

We have one understanding of fidelity intellectually and another emotionally—one for others and one for ourselves, and that is why it is upsetting to imagine sharing the person you love but easy to imagine loving more than one yourself. Men promise fidelity not so much because they want to be faithful, but because they hope the woman to whom they make the promise will then feel obliged to be so herself.

There are marriage partners who allow each other minutes out in other beds but forbid caring for anyone else, and others who allow each other soul-mates in abundance but forbid body-mates of any kind. And for each of those who have arrangements there are many couples more who operate on a speak-no-evil, hear-no-evil basis, making their minds up as their bodies go.

I have been furious with men who have expected me to be faithful, and I have been even more furious with those who did not, and once I screamed at a man whom I loved more than

I'd intended to, "If I'm faithful to you, what bloody business is it of yours?"

THE DREAM OF romantic love is taken more seriously in North America than it is anywhere else in the world, which is why we believe in fidelity and why we believe in infidelity as well. It is also, of course, what makes our divorce rate as high as it is. Falling in love at first sight and instant gratification are part of the world in which we live, so there are people who believe adamantly in fidelity. They just don't believe in it for long.

"What we love about love is the fever which marriage puts to bed and cures," Mignon McLaughlin wrote, and while that is a little hard to take for those who like to believe that everyone needs an understanding wife—so that they can forgive the man who occasionally chooses someone else's—it is nevertheless likely that it is true. You've just to read Ovid, who wrote before A.D., to see that men have been falling in love with other men's wives for a very long time. Some part of each of us is restless and that part cries out to be used, and trying to determine who is innocent and who is guilty is foolishness because all of us are both. Everyone is guilty of thinking there must be more—more excitement, more ego gratification, more status and more fulfillment—and everyone is innocent of the knowledge of what the more will cost.

JUDGING WHO IS faithful and who is not is not possible because no one knows what is in another's heart, and no two infidelities are the same.

A married couple decided to augment their relationship by permitting each other affairs with others. He had a few skirmishes which he told her about *en passant*, and after a while she became involved with a very important man whom he felt complemented by. She was concerned that he hadn't found anyone to spend his extra time with and, from time to time, mentioned her concern to her lover, by way of making it clear to him that her husband, not he, was the big love in her life. One day the lover told her that her husband had also found a secondary love, and when she heard this, she gave up the lover and her husband, the same day. Who is unfaithful? Is anyone faithful?

A couple went on their honeymoon and while away she was hospitalized and required treatment which resulted in a breast being removed. His family considered that her family had pawned off ersatz goods on their son and although he tried to accept things as they were he was clearly disappointed. Five or six years after the marriage he found she was having an affair and divorced her. Was she unfaithful to him? Or was he unfaithful to her?

A married man and a young girl had an affair and he alternately entreated her to give him up and to marry him, drinking more and becoming less rational with each entreaty. Ultimately it became clear he couldn't take much more of this and neither could she, so she ended the affair. He returned to his wife, appeared to stabilize himself, and when she next saw him *en famille* at a New Year's party he looked happy. As the bells rang the New Year in he tilted her head toward his and as their foreheads touched whispered, "I'll always love you but you knew that didn't you?" Does that mean he was faithful to her instead of to his wife? Who was the girl faithful to, if anybody?

If a man sleeps with his wife while thinking of his girlfriend, is he faithful to his wife? If he sleeps with his girlfriend and thinks of his wife, is he faithful to his wife? Who is to know? Often the man doesn't know himself.

PERHAPS IT WAS easier to be physically faithful in the Victorian era when everybody was supposed to be sexually repressed and bralessness did not abound, or in Frontier times perhaps, when life was tough and one didn't have food and clothes from all around the world beckoning in the stores and cars of a thousand kinds and colors demanding only a hundred dollars down. When it was calico or calico to dress in and buffalo stew or buffalo steak to eat, when a man was lucky to have one trusty horse and one trusty wife, perhaps it was easier to be faithful than it is today when a multiplicity of choices in every aspect of life makes it hard not to expect choices also in the one aspect of life that matters most.

There are those who say that the concept of fidelity was part of the Puritan ethic and hence is useless today, unless you still believe that "bruising the body will pleasure the soul." And there are those who feel it was a form of social control—intended to protect dependent mothers and babes and keep them from being a charge upon society—no longer necessary since sex has been liberated from conception for the first time since the dawn of time. Bertrand Russell felt we would do better to restrain our negative emotion, "jealousy," rather than our positive one, "loving," and there's a lot of sense in that. But I can remember a man who once asked me to run off into the sunset with him, for a day, or a week, or a night, and I remember saying I didn't think so, although part of me wanted to go. And when I told him that my reasons for refusing had largely to do with the fact that he wouldn't be around when I'd need him later, he testily replied, "Great ladies are not tied to their plumbing, nor do they expect men to play pool on the same table Tuesday and Friday for the rest of their lives." And I've been looking for those great ladies ever since he said that, but I haven't found one yet.

ONE OF THE problems of the new morality ushered in by the pill is that it doesn't have an equivalent for being in the man's tent the next morning chewing on his moccasins—or whatever used to be done—so while the pill has made women freer, it has also freed them to look after their psychosexual needs on their own. And many women who aspired to be "great ladies" found it wasn't so great to be one after all.

Sex deepens love and love deepens sex, so physical intimacy transforms everything and playing with it is playing with fire. Men try to ignore the fact that making love creates bonds, creating dependencies where there were none before, and women who try to ignore it with them deny their basic needs.

I'm not sure there can be loving without commitment, although commitment takes all kinds of forms, and there can be commitment for the moment as well as commitment for all time. The kind that is essential for loving marriages —and love affairs, as well—is a commitment to preserving the essential quality of your partner's soul, adding to them as a person rather than taking away. And if you haven't got that you haven't got loving, although you might have something else. You could have adventure or a postgraduate course, you might have rehabilitation, or a bit of gossamer to highlight an otherwise somber life, but you don't have loving, and of that you should be sure.

IF I HAD to choose between having someone physically faithful to me or having him committed to my preservation, I would opt for the latter because there is no doubt in my mind when I see couples at parties selling each other out which is the worst offense. Physical fidelity is a lovely thing if someone feels that way about you willingly, but relatively meaningless if you exact it for a price. And while it is easy enough to be faithful for the first five or ten years, it is more difficult by twice each year after that, so women as well as men are finding it hard to do.

There are problems connected with infidelity and problems connected with being faithful at any cost, and I am for letting those concerned choose the problems they'd prefer. There need not be one rule for all. Infidelity is enlarging and fragmenting and very very dangerous, but it has been known to retrieve people as well as marriages, so it can't be only bad. And while a lot of women would probably consider it better to have the man they care about rip-off other women if he must but hurry home again, I think I'd rather he be concerned about the survival of the people he sleeps with, even those who are not me. Men who take advantage of one woman take advantage of them all, and if he's going to have an experience in which I can't share, then I'd rather it be a good one, so if there are any benefits to trickle down the spout they'll be the kind I'd want.

If marriages are for the long haul, it follows that some decades are likely to be better than others, but when we used to think of marriages as forever, we accepted that better than we do today. In a short story I once read, a couple no longer young are out strolling on a summer's evening when they pass a house they'd once lived in now in the process of being demolished. And seeing the various wallpapers revealed by the wrecker's hammer, one reminds the other about the affair one of them was having when the rose paper was in the hall. Then they link arms again and stroll off on their way. Marriages change and adapt, rise and fall, circle and come about, but today most of us expect everything to be perfect each married day, so marriages fall prey to obsolescence as often as do cars.

We tend to think in terms of fixing blame, of establishing adultery and making clear who did what to whom, when what is most important is not what was done but that no one be hurt. It's not that we care that much if our mate rubs off

a few cells of epidermis in friction with someone else, it's that we are all afraid if he does,
he'll stop loving us. And men who've always
had affairs, considering it good for their mo-
rale, find that they are fearful just like their
wives when the shoe is on the other foot. Any
new ethic, if it's to work, will have to find ways
of reconciling growth with commitment, change
with loyalty, and freedom with alienation, because a world in which new loyalties constantly
replace old ones will make neurotics of us all.

A WOMAN I knew once told me that a man I
cared about and who cared about me also cared
about someone else, and although I knew the
facts she'd told me, since he had told me first,
it hurt to hear them from her. And I remember
wondering why it bothered me to learn what I
already knew, until it came to me that what I'd
lost was not innocence but face.

Maybe it is protection we are really asking
for when we ask for fidelity, social and emotional more than economic. Historically, fidelity
is considered most important when it is at-
tached to face-saving, and when it is not, jealousy seems to abate, which explains why the
French are able to have their *cinq à sept* hour
and why Moslem women and Chinese women
accepted their husbands' second and third wives
without apparent pain. Thoughtfulness and

commitment are the most important things, and if that's the case perhaps men who lie to their wives about their peccadilloes are more faithful than one would suppose.

I'VE LEARNED NOT to ask for everything, just to make sure that I get what I must have. It doesn't matter who else gets what—it only matters if you're deprived. Really splendid men understand that and find ways to manage their lives so they never give away anything that is their wife's. And if there are times when they need more than one woman in their life, they give back what they get to both. Being faithful means not costing people you love more than they can afford to pay. The best men are committed to their partners as much as to themselves.

PART FOUR

Alone

CHAPTER TEN

Loss
of Love

There was a girl once who worked for a newspaper and met a professor who was, or seemed
to be, everything she ever wanted. For a while
she flew to New York to meet him on weekends
and they stayed at a small hotel on the Park
and ate breakfast in the Palm Court, and sometimes, when his schedule permitted, he flew to
her city and played house with her and her
small son. Once he was trapped in her apart-

ment for five days by a snow storm that blan-
keted the whole east coast and, after he got over
his distress at not being able to teach his
classes, he said he thought he could really love
a girl who squeezed orange juice in the mornings in her housecoat and asked if she would
like to come to New York to meet his mom.

Being taken to meet someone's mother is the
big time whether you are sixteen or twenty-six,
so she bought a new dress and told her editor a
new excuse and flew off, filled with nice
thoughts, to their little hotel on the Park.

He was not expected to arrive till evening so
she went shopping for a new nightgown, and
she bought some flowers for their room, and
some more for him to give to his mother, and
was just stepping out of the bath when the
phone rang and a strange voice told her he
wasn't coming.

"He is tired," the voice, that of one of his
colleagues at the university, told her, "and too
strung out to make the trip into New York, so
he asked me to call you and say he has taken
some pills and gone to bed and will see you tomorrow around four." The man on the phone
sounded embarrassed and she felt sorry for him,
but she felt more sorry for herself and after
she hung up, she cried.

She tried calling his apartment after a bit,
but the phone was immediately picked up by
the answering service so she hung up; even
after she called them back and demanded that

they let her ring through, that didn't work and she began pacing around the room.

"What if he is sick?" she thought when she wasn't thinking "God damn him for not coming," and "Why didn't he at least call himself?" And then she lay down on the bed again and thought, "I can't possibly make it through to four tomorrow without speaking to him."

She thought of going to him, but she didn't know how to exactly, having only been there once or twice before and then always by air, so she called a lot of limousine companies listed under New England Transportation. And when they turned out to run only from the airport, she scrambled out of her nightie and into her new dress and took a cab to the bus terminal where she found the next bus left at 2:15 A.M.

The Port Authority was cold and sort of sinister at one in the morning and she shivered in her white coat and tried to avoid the eyes of the transient men who looked at her with curiosity. For an hour she sat huddled on a bench and wondered why she was there, and why she didn't go back to the hotel, or maybe even back to her own city. And, of course, she wondered what she would do if she found him with another girl. All the way out on the bus she thought, "Why am I doing this?" and went over in her mind what she would say to him when she got there, carefully rehearsing two sets of lines—one to say if he looked happy to see her and one to say if he looked horrified. By

the time she finally arrived in his town, she was
too tired to care what happened and part of her
hoped he'd have a blonde with him so she would
know for sure he was a cad. Then the bus
dropped her off at a street corner and there
wasn't a cab anywhere and she got lost walking
to his apartment, which she knew only by its
proximity to their favorite hamburger restau-
rant. When she did find it, he didn't hear her
knocking for a long time and she was afraid
someone rising early might see her trying to
get into his apartment and she was also afraid
he was deliberately not answering her knock.

When he did answer the door, rubbing his
eyes heavy with sleep and looking like he
couldn't quite remember who she was, she forgot both lines she had planned to say all the
way up in the bus, and finally blurted out, "I
am bloody glad both of us are writers because
somebody better get some mileage out of this
stinking night somehow," and he let her in. She
took off her new dress, now wrinkled, and
crawled into his tiny bed with her knees tucked
up to her stomach and her face to the wall and
after a while he got up and splashed cold water
in his eyes to undo the effect of the sleeping
pills and made love to her while she shivered.

In the morning they took the train to New
York and they went to see his mother and when
he left her in the morning, after another night
in their little hotel, he said, "If you asked me if
it were now or never I'd say never, but I do be-

lieve it is you and I, somewhere, someplace,
baby," and then he smiled one of his marvelous
smiles and jumped into a cab and she never saw
him again.

NOTHING HURTS WORSE than the end of a love
affair unless perhaps it is the time just before
the end. "There is a way of leaving and not
leaving," Cyril Connolly wrote in *The Unquiet
Grave*, "of hinting that one loves and is willing
to return yet never coming back. Someone who
knows how to prolong this state and to repro-
duce it at will can be quite insignificant—and
so is the sand wasp which stings a grub in the
nerve centre where it will be paralyzed yet re-
main alive."

Psychologists have a way of making rats
psychotic by ringing a bell and patting them,
and then ringing a bell and feeding them, and
when the rats learn to run over, tails wagging,
when the bell rings, belting them one instead,
until the rats both fear and love the bell and go
out of their little furry minds.

Men who fear loving are like those sand
wasps and like the psychologists who torment
rats, because they want love and ask for it, but
when it comes they draw back. The more one
wants love, the more terrifying loving is because it threatens so much need, so men who
are most in need of love are the first to run.

When you are wooing someone, you're in charge, but if you allow yourself to really love them and be loved as well, you're no longer in control, and that is what they fear. Men who fear loving move on once the first stage of love is over because they like to stop while they're ahead. And men who slip away slowly, smiling as they go, are leaving just as surely as those who run away, although those who move more quickly leave less hurt in their wake.

AND WHAT HAPPENS when the love affair has ended and you're alone and unloved? The symptoms, so personal, so horrible, are nevertheless universal, and there are few among us who don't know them by heart—although no one to whom they are happening can believe anyone else ever suffered as much.

Six about-turns of the mind each half-hour—all lived with the desperation of a poker player who is losing badly and keeps playing for higher and higher stakes hoping to win it all back. Fantasies of revenge, do-si-doing with plots of how to convince him you will change. Fevers and convulsions interspersed with blessed moments of remission in which you say quietly to yourself, "I'll show him," only to start crying again.

The overwhelming feelings of worthlessness, the days and even weeks of lying on the bed, not eating, not caring about anything, willing yourself dead, but too apathetic to take any action to stop living. Perhaps drinking too much or smoking all the time. Interminable nights punctuated by 3:00 A.M. drives along deserted expressways while the car radio plays sad songs. All songs are sad now—even the happy ones. Desperate, shameless calls to friends and all too often to him. Mornings when sunshine makes you pull the covers up over your head and days at work when the voice catches at the most inopportune moments. All of this with a feeling in the pit of your stomach akin to being in an elevator from which the floor has just fallen.

And what of the friends who try to help, impotent except for good intentions? Should they say, "He's not worth it," what a surprise they get when you hotly defend him. Should he not have been worth it, then what would that make you for having believed in him? You might be able in time to part with him, but parting with the dream of having been loved or having loved is something else again. To give up loving means to go back to being closed, and people whom love has opened fear that if it goes they'll never be able to open up again. Sometimes they feel that if they lose this person, they'll never again be able to love, so they hold on to the dream of them, loving their dream, long after the love object itself is gone.

I remember an extraordinarily handsome

public relations executive talking of the months
that followed his breakup with a girl he'd been
living with, and saying, in a voice that was
barely audible although ten years had passed,
"I didn't go to work, I didn't shave, I never left
my apartment except to buy milk for the instant coffee I lived on, and at night I'd drive all
the way to where Susan was staying with her
parents, and I'd sit outside in my car and cry,
and then I'd drive all the way back home again.
A couple of times I did it twice in one night.
Finally I knocked on the front door one morning, after I'd sat there all night, and told her
mother I would not go away until Susan came
back to live with me. And I went back to the
car and sat there for another day and a half
until she came out with a suitcase and we went
home and she stayed with me for another half
a year. I would have died in that car—I didn't
care—I was half frozen by the time she came
out."

FOURTEEN OR FORTY, nobody is immune. We all
feel the same sense of desperation when love is
withdrawn. And success in other areas doesn't
make it any easier when somebody you want
doesn't want you. Even when the whole thing
has been over for months or even years, lovers
often speak of walking by the former lover's
house or looking for their car unconsciously in

parking lots and even going back to places they used to go to together. News of the former lover is very often obsessionally sought and treasured and beautiful weather seems to make many abandoned lovers desperate, as if nice days are wasted when they can't be shared. The hours just before twilight are a desperate time, too, when the daylight begins to fail and abandoned lovers must accept the fact that they have no one to plan the evening around. And physical similarities, of course, do it to us all. A smile, perhaps, or the way someone brushes their hair back, and the lover jumps across the mindscreens. What a masochistic lot unrequited lovers are. But who can blame them? There is no worse hell, and very few of us act better when it is our turn.

Some say it is the rejection itself that panics us and that it hasn't a thing to do with how much the lover was valued. And that seems likely, as many of us have wept copious tears over someone we were planning to leave ourselves before they beat us to it.

Perhaps it is the loss of the dream of being loved and loving that matters more than the loss of the lover himself, and that is a loss of self. One can't run in a park without a dog or make angels in the snow without a child and there are things one can't do without a lover, so the loss of the lover is like an amputation and the patient goes into shock. And sometimes because it has happened once it keeps happen-

ing again. Many people who'd feared that their
lover might leave them found that he ultimately
did.

IT CAN TAKE years to get over a broken love affair, and maybe one never really does. Popular
wisdom has it that one must keep busy and,
while a new project or a new dress isn't really
the answer, there isn't really an answer, so we
try them and in time things don't seem as bad.

It helps to have a friend who walks you
around as one would do for somebody who has
taken an overdose of sleeping pills, walks you
to lunch and to movies despite your protests,
and keeps you moving until the life-preserving
juices start once more to flow.

And, of course, if keeping busy, and time and
a little help from your friends makes it easier,
so does finding someone else. It's a little like the
hair of the dog that bit you, of course, but then,
as John O'Hara observed, Where would love be
without loneliness?

CHAPTER ELEVEN

When Marriage Ends

A woman whom I used to know once put a husband through college and raised a couple of kids and when the children went to school took a job, fearing that her husband thought her dull. And when she'd become successful at the thing she did, her husband left her for his secretary and she wished that she could die. There is a moral to this story, although it is not the one that comes to mind at first—although we're

taught that women who opt for success forfeit
being loved—after this woman dried her eyes,
another man fell in love with her and after a
while she found she loved him more.

"IF THE SECOND marriage is a success the first
one really isn't a failure," Mignon McLaughlin
wrote, and lots of people who were left by someone once, ultimately wonder why they ever
stayed themselves. It is not easy to tell the bad
luck from the good luck, and sometimes things
that look about as bad as they can be when they
first happen, turn out to be good luck after
you've lived with them awhile.

Some people are part of the problem and
some are part of the solution, some roads lead
forward, and some lead back. And while it feels
terrible to be upended by someone who wants a
new life—giving you yours back in the process
—husbands who interpret the change of life as
being the time they trade in their forty-year-
old wife for two twenties are victims of a sort,
themselves.

We all want to be eternally youthful, enchanted and enchanting each and every day,
and sometimes men as well as women make the
mistake of believing that when they start to
lose their glow, it has to be their spouses' fault.
Men particularly are the victims of a society
that associates virility and youthfulness with

winning new territory rather than with protecting what you've got, so some go out to hunt when they're not really discontent, making divorce one of the major causes of divorce.

Men who need women who make them feel young make it very hard for women to grow old, and since that's something we all have no choice but to do, there is no way to please this kind of man. Marriages based on the notion that women are sex objects and must be decorative tend to die when the woman outgrows that role, either by becoming older or by becoming wiser—it is all the same. But a new crop of men who value women as people is growing up today, and for every marriage of the old type that doesn't survive, another of the new will take its place someday.

ONE OF THE fringe benefits of being handed back your life is being awarded custody of yourself. And while society often sees women whose husbands left them as the victims of divorce, if the wife starts to grow again she's the one who has been given the second chance, while a husband who hopes to find eternal youth by subduing yet another woman is still playing the same old game.

When you are first on your own, it may not seem a lucky break, because it takes time to rediscover who you are. (And when you are used

to defining yourself as half of a couple, or as
the wife of a particular man, it takes a while to
get this clear.) Most women, when they first
find themselves alone again, unconsciously wait
for another man to define themselves around,
remaking themselves a little for each one that
comes along.

The fear of being on one's own panics some
people so much they stay with a marriage well
after it's left them, pretending that the dream
still lives, for family and for friends, for con-
vention and morality, and because it's hard to
face the truth and with it the painful quality of
growth, the loneliness of life without one's
dreams, without the familiar, and without the
public approval one fears will be withdrawn.

It is awful to be rejected but there is pain in
rejecting too, and not having your needs met is
no worse than meeting those of others out of
guilt or fear instead of love. There is pain in
allowing yourself to be destroyed, and living in
a graveyard of broken dreams. And when there
are no more compromises to make, no more
hopes you can forsake, there is pain in giving
up.

Vast expanses of one's potential for feeling
are crushed in a bad marriage, and there are
people who never want to risk being hurt again,
but when you finally accept that the end has
come and begin to go about your life there is
rejuvenation in discovering yourself. And while
at times it feels a little like a second adoles-

cence, like standing on quicksand where nothing is safe, in time you get used to it and take pride in belonging to yourself.

OUR GRANDPARENTS STAYED together at all costs and sometimes the cost was great, so we are lucky that we can restructure our lives. Divorce is very expensive, both economically and psychologically as well, but it probably isn't any more so than living with someone who isn't really on your side. And since there are alternatives today to being married, for women as well as for men, more people will divorce.

It used to be that it was men who asked for the divorce and women who tried to hold their marriages together, because when marriages broke up wives lost more than just their husbands—they lost their jobs as well. But today women no longer have to be married to express their sexuality with changing mores and the pill. A woman with a career has an identity and an economic base of her own, so more women who don't think they are being treated fairly are leaving home. And men who meant to love, honor and support, but didn't get around to it quite yet, are doing their supporting, but through the courts.

We once rewarded wives' sacrifices and shored up marriages as we did, but today we tend to look askance at housewives, so there are a lot of women who feel they'd be respected more if they were on their own. Women who once married to have the role of wife and mother, and the status that went with that, are finding that being a wife today costs them as much as it gives them—and the highest cost is an identity of their own.

ONCE THE ONLY people concerned with divorce were those divorced themselves, but today divorce is all around us and the large number of divorces makes the whole society less stable, affecting the married and the divorced alike. It is a tantalizing world we live in and one that makes all things seem possible and sometimes more exciting than they really are. And so married women, like married men, often feel they are missing out, and many of them will pitch the baby out with the bathwater only to find they've exchanged one set of problems for another not appreciably better than the first.

Divorce doesn't solve anything any more than marriage does—you have to do that yourself. And women who hoped their husbands would take care of everything and then turned cool when they found that he could not, would be wiser if they parted with their illusions instead of with their husbands. Because after you're divorced, you're still stuck with yourself.

THE PRICE FOR those Fifties marriages is in, and it is higher than any of us expected it to be. And while there are many who find it shocking that women are now considering their own needs instead of only those of babes and men, it is not a bad thing that they are. Many women who sacrificed their own growth for their families' were both a cause and a casualty of their divorces. Nobody really wants to spend life with someone who has no other choice, and children who have been raised by a mother who gave up her life for them almost always spend years on an analyst's couch learning to spit in her eye.

WE USED TO see divorce as an evil, and divorcing people as wicked and selfish, and then we came to see them more as failures than as sinners and dropped our hostility to them to become patronizing instead. All of which, of course, affects how divorcing people see themselves, so too many of them are filled with bitterness, guilt and doubt.

The time has come for us to view divorce in a more positive way, because whether we like the idea or not it is no longer an isolated event. Man is not naturally monogamous, so good marriages don't turn up every day even when we wish they would. And it doesn't make much sense to think of one person as the bad guy and the other as the innocent victim, nor does it help either of them much. No marriage is one person's failure any more than it's one person's success, so it works best to see a marriage that has ended simply as something that didn't work out. If you don't blame yourself, it is easier not to blame your former spouse, and since none of us is perfect nobody should expect us to be, especially ourselves. It is not necessary to devalue the past and find it spurious because it doesn't last forever, it is possible to simply go on to what's next. If there are no endings, there are no beginnings and you see no new lands, so for everything that's lost, there is usually something gained.

CHAPTER TWELVE

On Your Own

Living alone is a life without mirrors, a life without a diary to read to see where you have been. And if at times it seems as if nothing has really happened, when it hasn't been recorded by another set of eyes, it is also true that when you stop relying on others to tell you what they see, you see for yourself and clearer still.

While single women may not have a man they can count on or call at four in the night, they do have the knowledge that when a man comes to see them he wants to be with them. And while he may come less often, he will really be there when he does. On the nights he doesn't come, the single woman can do the things she chooses to do. She has no laundry to do as tithes to pay for these special moments, no business acquaintances to entertain, no sports events to grudgingly sit through, no school buddies to tolerate, so the nights he does not come are her nights—nights to grow, alone or with others, nights to dream replenishing dreams. Her apartment can be decorated with chintz instead of corduroy, her vacation may be by the sea, and she can spend her money any way she chooses, instead of the way he thinks best.

There are many fringe benefits to being alone. You tend to have far more real, intense friendships when you are single, perhaps because you can be more honest when you do not have the marriage or someone else's feelings to protect. That means friends can share a larger part of you, and you of them as well, and friendships can be really intimate rather than activity-oriented associations that only meet to do some special thing.

If one of the problems of marriage is that safety can lead to complacency, then one of the advantages of being single is that one is never safe enough to grow complacent, and constantly having to prove oneself often leads to growth.

Being alone means swimming in many waters, and that can mean a more interesting life. And if it is true that a single woman hasn't got one man she can count on, it is also true that, by living on the fringe of many men's lives, she is privy to many ideas and interests denied most married women—and indeed most men. Men tell women to whom they are not married truths they cannot tell their wives and fear to tell to men, and what one learns one day from one man makes you more interesting the next day for another—as well as for yourself.

There were women in the golden age of Greece, called *hetaerae*, who were celebrated by Socrates and philosophers of his time. Although they existed solely for their own pleasure and that of men, they were respected for their independence of mind and spirit and thought of highly by the Greeks. Single women in today's world can function like *hetaerae*, learning from many and giving back to whom they will, and for the woman who enjoys such a life, it can be a good one, and one both she and society can be the better for.

While married women must adapt to the perimeters of their marriages, single women can expand in all directions, developing as they will. Women who have realized themselves make good companions, and women as well as men find associations with them rewarding and fun—not only because they are more often interesting but because they haven't grown neurotic making a virtue of doing what they most dislike. And time with them is generally given freely, little asked in return.

I REMEMBER WHEN I was first married how important it was to me that my husband find me beautiful, talented, womanly and bright. And when he didn't always, I was not these things—as if he'd turned off my light. After we parted and went on to other lives, from time to time a man thought me beautiful and occasionally another found me bright. Until in time I was those things even when no one was around, and today because they're mine I can give them to whomever I choose. Women who have had a chance to find out who they are don't need as much reassurance from men, having come to terms with themselves, and while it is always nicer to be around people who see you as you want to see yourself, you can't be done in as easily by ones who don't.

There is a lot to be said for being single—and more today than ever before. It is a new world we are living in now, and although there are rules for virginal females under eighteen and for married ones twenty to eighty-five, there are no rules for single women, so we are able to make our own.

IT'S NO LONGER necessary to see being single as an underprivileged state. In a world where women don't have to marry for economic support, status or identity, being single is going to become more common and hence more easily done. But if it is a mistake to see being single as a state of deprivation, it is just as much a mistake to romanticize it and claim it is only good.

Single women have more moonlit drives and weekends out of town, but they may often spend their birthdays on their own and sometimes when they want to see a movie they have to take themselves. Married women plan to do things "after the children finish school" or "when we take two weeks in the summer," but it is more difficult to plan when you're alone and your whole world could change twice before tomorrow and then change back again.

Men advance and recede on a moon cycle of their own as every woman knows, so there are times when a single woman leads a very exciting life and times when she has no one for company but herself. It is seasonal work being single and you never know how long your season will be, nor can you direct whether spring will follow winter. You just have to wait and hope and see.

The intellectual appeal of being liberated is strong but the old emotional conditioning is stronger still, so the time between men can be like the moments when you step down off the merry-go-round and the world is out of sync. It's a time when you live in the shadows between what you thought you wanted and what you will ultimately get, and for those who can remember resenting waiting for a man to come home from work it doesn't help to learn it's even worse when you don't have one for whom to wait.

You can be as much at the mercy of men outside of marriage as within it, and women who've gone from their fathers' houses to their husbands' find it hard to make decisions without a man in mind. You are much more vulnerable when you are alone and much more up for grabs, and while you multiply your chances for the serendipitous encounter, you multiply your potential problems too. It can be a richer life intellectually and socially when you are on your own, but emotionally it's hit and miss. There is only one thing worse than being used and that's not being used, so in periods of drought single women have to take their risks.

It is harder to keep your emotional supply lines well secured when you are single—and we all have needs for safety, for closeness, and for respect—so lack of intimacy often leads to alienation and alienation leads to lack of intimacy for good. And because women who elect to go it alone today are doing spadework for a world that does not yet exist, there are as many brutalized and embittered among the single as among the badly married, and this will not quickly change.

The world is divided into couples, and so being single can feel like playing musical chairs and every time they stop the music, you're the one who's out. When you are alone, you are out there—single, apart, and exposed—and married people have been known to find that threatening, so they isolate you more. Sometimes they make you an object onto which they transfer their hostilities or their fantasies or both, like the married men who flirt with you to show their wives a thing or two. And while that is their problem and hasn't a lot to do with you, it can hurt as much or more than if it did. I am sure it's safer somehow when there is someone in your camp, to help you fight the battles, and I am just as sure that when there is, there are fewer of them to fight.

You don't have anyone on whom you can make demands when you are on your own, and very often you get tired of being brave. So while there are single women who are wary and others who smile most of the time, both learn very quickly not to give away anything they can't part with easily, without having to ask for something back.

I sleep in a fourposter bed and have a glamorous job, and I buy the clothes I want to, and talk to interesting people on a white phone but there are times when I am totally alone. And sometimes when I meet married women at parties who ask me what it's like to work in television or if I've ever met Cary Grant, it isn't difficult to see that some of them wish they had my life and that they sometimes feel the only thing keeping them from realizing their dreams of fame and fortune is that their husbands expect them to be at home at night. And even though I know a lot of things they fortunately won't have to learn, some part of me envies them their innocence, and there are days when I would trade what I have for that.

"TWO FEARS ALTERNATE," Cyril Connolly wrote in *The Unquiet Grave*, "the one of loneliness and the other of bondage," so when we are bound we yearn for freedom and when we are free we think of nothing but our loneliness. This imbalance is in all of us, so we are never completely satisfied. When we have one thing we will always wish we had the other, although those who are aware that this is so have a better chance of avoiding over-reacting to their own reactions, and that is something of a help.

Single women often envy married ones and dream of being married themselves, while married women fantasize about holding court for marvelous men if only they were free. But the dreams of the married about being single rarely include being lonely, and when the single think about being married they think of being happily married only. And since the gods have a way of giving some of us all of one thing while others get a lot of another, the *Sturm und Drang* of the single life looks exciting to those who are quietly settled, and contentment looms large and elusive to those who've had more emotion than they can take but very little quiet joy.

I have been married and I have been single and I guess I'd have to say it's a half dozen of one thing and six of another and it really depends on what suits you best and when. Those who choose to keep their ears open to the promptings of their own destiny will always pay a price, but for many of them the price will be right. It needn't really be a choice between being a free woman who's alone more than she chooses, and a vassal exhausted by the demands of others who never guess that she has needs herself. If we try, in the not too distant future, there could be free women who are married and married women who are free, as well as men who rejoice in them and love them more each day. There are very few women who are tough enough to be soft and many women have turned against their own needs today because they've seen the price some women have had to pay for theirs. We are all very frightened of love's power to create and destroy but if there were men who were capable of valuing the best that women have in them, women would always be glad to love them.

There are no perfect men of course, but some are more perfect than others, and we can use all of those we can get. It's true that there are fewer reasons to marry than there were in our parents' day, but the most important one remains the same. It is still awfully nice to have someone to curl around in the night.

ABOUT THE AUTHOR

MERLE SHAIN graduated as a social worker and practiced for several years as a case worker, mostly in the field of family counseling. In recent years, she has worked in the media—first in radio as a writer and broadcaster, and then in television as a story editor, interviewer, hostess and critic. She was a feature writer for the newspaper *The Toronto Telegram*, and Associate Editor of *Chatelaine*, Canada's women's magazine. In 1968, she was on Prime Minister Trudeau's staff during his successful bid for the Liberal Party leadership.

She has been married and has a son, and lives in Toronto.

Author of

**Some Men Are More
Perfect Than Others**

MERLE
SHAIN

is now available for lectures through
the BANTAM LECTURE BUREAU.

For further details, contact:

Bantam
On Psychology

- [ ] BLACK RAGE, William H. Grier, M.D. and
  Price M. Cobbs, M.D. — 3931 • .95
- [ ] THE FIFTY-MINUTE HOUR, Robert Lindner — 4388 • .95
- [ ] PSYCHOANALYSIS AND RELIGION, Erich Fromm — 5558 • .95
- [ ] THE PSYCHOLOGY OF SELF-ESTEEM: A New Concept of
  Man's Psychological Nature, Nathaniel Branden — 5712 • $1.25
- [ ] BREAKING FREE, Nathaniel Branden — 7002 • $1.25
- [ ] THE JESUS BAG, William H. Grier, M.D. and Price M.
  Cobbs, M.D. — 7188 • $1.25
- [ ] PSYCHO-CYBERNETICS AND SELF-FULFILLMENT,
  Maxwell Maltz, M.D. — 7286 • $1.50
- [ ] GESTALT THERAPY VERBATIM, Fritz Perls — 7292 • $1.65
- [ ] IN AND OUT THE GARBAGE PAIL, Fritz Perls — 7299 • $1.65
- [ ] GOING CRAZY: THE RADICAL THERAPY OF R. D. LAING,
  Dr. Hendrik Ruitenbeek, ed. — 7352 • $1.65
- [ ] THE DISOWNED SELF, Nathaniel Branden — 7502 • $1.50
- [ ] THE MIND GAME: WITCHDOCTORS AND PSYCHIATRISTS,
  E. Fuller Torrey — 7657 • $1.50
- [ ] WHAT DO YOU SAY AFTER YOU SAY HELLO? Eric Berne, M.D. — 7711 • $1.95
- [ ] NUTRITION AND YOUR MIND: The Psychochemical
  Response, George Watson — 7793 • $1
- [ ] AWARENESS: exploring, experimenting, experiencing,
  John O. Stevens — 8053 • $1.5
- [ ] STRANGERS TO THEMSELVES: Readings on Mental Illness,
  Gene and Barbara Stanford, eds. — 8267 • $1.25
- [ ] PSYCHOSOURCES, A Psychology Resource Catalog,
  Evelyn Shapiro, ed. — 8501 • $5.00

Buy them at your local bookstore or use this handy coupon for ordering:

Bantam Books, Inc., Dept. ME, 414 East Golf Road, Des Plaines, Ill. 60016

Please send me the books I have checked above. I am enclosing $_____
(please add 35¢ to cover postage and handling). Send check or money order
—no cash or C.O.D.'s please.

Mr/Mrs/Miss_____

Address_____

City_____ State/Zip_____

ME—7/74

Please allow three weeks for delivery. This offer expires 7/75.

RELAX!

SIT DOWN
and Catch Up On Your Reading!

FREE!
Bantam Book Catalog

It lists over a thousand money-saving bestsellers originally priced from $3.75 to $15.00 —bestsellers that are yours now for as little as 50¢ to $2.95!

The catalog gives you a great opportunity to build your own private library at huge savings!

So don't delay any longer—send for your catalog TODAY! It's absolutely FREE!